T

READING PEOPLE

Observes body language, learn human behavior and read persons like a book. How to Analyze anyone and decode their Intentions by using your deepest mental skills

LIAM ROBINSON

Congratulations on purchase This book and thank You for doing so.

Please enjoy!

© Copyright 2021 by **LIAM ROBINSON**

<u>All rights reserved</u>

DISCLAIMER

No part of this publication may be reproduced, distributed, or transmitted in any form or by any means, including photocopying, recording, or other electronic or mechanical methods, or by any information storage and retrieval system without the prior written permission of the publisher, except in the case of very brief quotations embodied in critical reviews and certain other noncommercial uses permitted by copyright law.

PRINTED IN USA

MIND MASTERY SERIES

If you have come to this eBook without having read the previous parts, I suggest you do so in order to have an overall reading. Below is the correct titles, if you would like to search for them on <u>Amazon and/or Audible</u>:

<u>SECRET MANIPULATION TECHNIQUES</u>

HOW SUBLIMINAL PSYCHOLOGY CAN PERSUADE ANYONE BY APPLYING DARK PNL IN REAL-LIFE. UNDERSTANDING TACTICS & SCHEMES TO INFLUENCE PEOPLE AND CONTROL THEIR EMOTIONS

<u>HOW TO ANALYZE PEOPLE WITH DARK PSYCHOLOGY</u>

A SPEED GUIDE TO READING HUMAN PERSONALITY TYPES BY ANALYZING BODY LANGUAGE. HOW DIFFERENT BEHAVIORS ARE MANIPULATED BY MIND CONTROL

HOW TO SPEED READ PEOPLE

READING HUMAN BODY LANGUAGE TO UNDERSTAND PSYCHOLOGY AND DARK SIDE OF THE PERSONS – HOW TO ANALYZE BEHAVIORAL EMOTIONAL INTELLIGENCE FOR THE MIND CONTROL

EMOTIONAL INTELLIGENCE MASTERY

DISCOVER HOW EQ CAN MAKE YOU MORE PRODUCTIVE AT WORK AND STRENGTHEN RELATIONSHIPS. IMPROVE YOUR LEADERSHIP SKILLS TO ANALYZE & UNDERSTAND OTHER PEOPLE THROUGH EMPATHY

NLP MASTERY

HOW TO ANALYZE DARK PSYCHOLOGY TECHNIQUES TO CHANGE YOUR HABITS AND BUILD A SUCCESSFUL LIFE. ESSENTIAL GUIDE ON MIND CONTROL THROUGH CALIBRATING EMOTIONAL INTELLIGENCE AND HIDDEN EMOTIONS

*"For better enjoyment, you CAN find all this titles also in audio format, on **Audible**."*

Table of Contents

Introduction

Chapter 1: Read People Like Book

How to Read Body Language

How Reading People Can Help You Make More Sales

Learn How by Using Your Mind Skills
- I see what you say
- Setting Up The Exercise

Chapter 2: People-Readers Are Dealmakers

- THE LOGIC MAN
- Possible Issues
- THE ACTION MAN
- Possible Problems
- THE FEELING INDIVIDUAL
- Possible Problems
- THE FUN Man
- Possible Problems

Do Associations Create Our Perceptions Of People?
- Conditioning
- The Ego Mind
- The Benefits
- The Halo Effect
- Inaccurate Associations

- Countries and Religions
- The Younger Generation
- Men And Women
- Absolute Meaning
- Awareness

How to Read a Person from Their Personal Hygiene

Body Language Speaks Without Words

Women's Body Language

Common Non-Verbal Mistakes

Chapter 3: Building Your Listening Skills

How to discover Confidence

The Communicating Confidence Guide

When You are Betrayed by Body Language

Chapter 4: How Body Language Improves Your Mindset

How our body speaks

Four different ways you can change your body language

Collapsing your arms

Force presenting

Quit slumping

HE TRIES TO MAINTAIN A VERY STRICT EXPRESSION ON HIS FACE ALL OF THE TIME.

Understanding Non-verbal Signals

Troublesome Conversations and Defensiveness

Establishing a Confident First Connection

Public Speaking

Chapter 5: Personality Types

1. The Know It All
2. The Sniper
3. The Yes Person
4. The No Man
6. The Grenade
7. The Whiner
8. The Tank
9. The Think They Know It All
10. The Blank Wall

Chapter 6: Manipulation

Psychological manipulation

The most effective method to Stop Manipulation in the Workplace

How to manipulate girlfriend

Conclusion

INTRODUCTION

It's about understanding, beyond words, what other people intend to say. It has to do with sensing what they genuinely mean, even when they say otherwise. The ability to assess individuals correctly will significantly influence your social, individual, and job life. When you understand just how another individual is feeling, you can adapt your message and communication style to ensure it is presented in the best way possible. It's not that difficult. This might appear difficult, but you don't require any type of special powers to recognize precisely how to read people.

Though it would give a lot of benefits, due to the highly competitive and ruthless situation that prevails in all fields, it's unethical to read people's minds. But Reading people's body language comes perilously close. The methods must be regularly learned so that the results are near perfect. It's an accepted fact that you can figure out what the person is thinking by watching a person's body language and eye movements.

In reality, reading the signs of body language and eye movements is a great skill and you can do a lot with it if it is mastered. Of course, many people should have this ability, but many of us are not paying attention to the messages that emanate through these skills from other people. You need to start paying more attention to these things if you want to utilize this ability.

Observing eye movements is a good way to start to read people's minds. Experts have discovered that if a person looks upwards and to the left, they are attempting to create an image in their thoughts. If a person looks up and right, you can see that he or she is trying to remember a specific image.

Another point is that nervous people or those who tell lies will not stare at another person's face. You can't expect the person to look at you specifically if the person is nervous or timid, they just can't keep their eyes on you. Confident people, on the other hand, retain their eye contact for a longer period. The same is true for lovers.

If someone wants to get close to you, if you move closer to them, they will respond positively. They're going to stay where they are or try to get a little closer still. They're going to retract a little or step away from the scene if they don't want you to get closer to them emotionally. If the person agrees with you while speaking, their knees will be pointed at you. If the knees are turned away from you, on the contrary, you may infer that anything you say is not acceptable to them. Similarly, people who are anxious or restless continue to shift their weight and lift their feet. When you watch a person sitting uncross his or her arms, you can quickly see that he or she is an easygoing person.

The location of the head will also help you determine what people think. Tilted heads show sympathy for you. A tilted head with a smile on the face shows he or she is a friendly person or can be perceived as a flirting message. Then, when speaking, the person lowers his or her head, you can be sure he or she is trying to hide something.

Many people are going to try to copy your behavior. It means they're interested in you and they're trying to build a friendship with you. You can make any changes to your actions to test it, and if they also try to imitate these changes, you can be sure that they are very interested in you. You should also watch the arms motion to read the mind of a man. If the individual folds them around the chest or crosses his or her arms, they may be trying to shield themselves from the effects of others. With such crossed arms, when they keep their feet wider, these people display their strength. When you keep your hands on the breasts, you may say that they become impatient. We prove that they are not averse to conversations by holding their fists behind them.

You must not be overly concerned with reading other people's parts. If you're too zealous, others will figure out you're trying to find out what they're non-verbally talking about or trying to read them. They're going to get a little formal with you. This can ruin your friendship with individuals. Therefore, when you try to read men, you must follow a subtle approach.

This is just the introduction to learning the art of reading people. There is so much more to it. You will learn not only how to read verbal and non-verbal cues, but also to read their psyche and to learn how to manipulate and how not to be manipulated with these cues. Keep reading. You've got a lot to learn.

CHAPTER 1: READ PEOPLE LIKE BOOK

Figure out how to read people like a book, and with other people, you'll be able to achieve so much more. Once you understand what's going on inside them, you can manipulate them, persuade them and even control them with your mind.

The way you do this is by trying to understand certain patterns of personality and how they organize their inner experience. You can, for instance, determine if someone is a person who can handle pressure well, or, even in stressful situations, can keep his cool.

There are three key ways in which people respond to stress: mental, decision, or thought. Emotional people are the ones that get plunged into some emotions and can't do anything about it. Thoughtful people are those who first encounter the emotions, but then choose to separate themselves from them and objectively work through them. And then some have no emotional response at all - they only respond rationally, objectively, then think things right away.

One way you can do this is to remind them about a work situation in which they had trouble going through. In reality, emotional people are going to revive the experience to some degree - you can hear the emotions in their tone of voice, you can see how the muscles in their faces can shift, their body posture, or movements.

You could initially see that thoughtful people will look for a moment but then they go back into a neutral state. Yet "thinkers" will not go into feelings at all, and they will simply recite the truth. Now, reading this may seem like thinkers are the best type to be in, but it depends on what kind of situation. For example, many of the best cooks in the world seem to be emotional people - and that's no accident because they need to think, feel and experience things to be good in their line of work.

Nevertheless, a surgeon should be a thinker rather than a highly emotional person.

And when it comes to counseling jobs or roles where communication skills are needed, "choosers" or thoughtful people are usually best because they can react emotionally to the concerns of another person but they can also see the rational side of it. So when you're in a situation with high stress, for instance, you might be able to help an anxious person by saying: "Can you imagine how we'll feel about this situation two years from now when we look back on all of this?" This allows them to disassociate themselves from the situation.

Different approaches can work more efficiently depending on what type of person you are speaking to. Often, if you want emotional people to be inspired, use emotional words to make them excited. Using terms such as "mind-boggling," "extraordinary," "intense."

You can use phrases for "choosers" such as: "This isn't just exciting and fun, it also makes a lot of sense." And for "thinkers," you're just presenting the hard facts. Mention figures, speak of "clear thinking" and "cold reality."

As you can see, learning to read people like a book takes some practice - but once you get to know the right language, you can use this ability to easily control other people.

HOW TO READ BODY LANGUAGE

There are two ways in which you can use body language to improve your face-to-face interactions: by studying the person's body language and regulating your body language. Knowing what others tell you by their non-verbal communication and taking control of the messages you receive, you can improve your communication skills. The actions and reactions of your body speak louder than words. It's all about knowing what to look for.

Positive non-verbal interaction is generally very effective as an indication of how a person feels without exaggerating gestures. A negative response is indicated by excessive interaction. Non-verbal negative actions are less effective. Actions most often perceived as negative can simply reflect the level of comfort, level of energy, or personal diversion. When you notice what you believe is negative body language, don't jump to conclusions.

HOW READING PEOPLE CAN HELP YOU MAKE MORE SALES

Welcome to the first chapter of 'Become a Sales Guru' using NLP and hypnotic methods. Here you'll learn skills that will bring your sales to the next stage and boost your progress.

Consider this before we go further:

Would you like to know why your customers make purchasing decisions so you can sell them in their 'own' language?

Want to ask some little questions that will give you the ultimate insight to please your customers best?

Do you want to reduce buyer's shame?

Would you like more business to be created and more referrals?

How useful would it be to know how to use your language to prevent objections?

Would that be helpful?

First, I want to lay down some ground rules:

- All methods will be used in an ethical manner and with dignity.
- You're going to apply these skills because the information is useless without practice.
- Just have fun with it. It's a win-win situation. It's just great for everyone involved.

Are we agreed?

In this first section, I would like to give you an ability that will allow you to pick up on whether your message is getting through, which will cause you to become brilliant while reading people, thus anticipating objections, etc. When you find that your message is not getting through, you must be able to change your tactics to be successful. If you can master this, then in the sales arena, you will become a god and be respected by everyone.

So let's explore Sensory Acuity.

What is Sensory Acuity?

When NLP first started, the founders wanted to model the late Dr. Milton H. Erickson, the psychologist who brought hypnosis off the stage and into common medical practice.

Now what we found about Dr. Erickson was that from moment to moment he had an amazing ability to recognize subtle changes in people and that with enough 'sensory acuity', those subtle changes have meaning.

Therefore, sensory acuity involves paying attention to the person with whom you interact and recognizing the subtle changes that occur in their body language. In learning how to do this, you'll be able to know if it's time to close a sale or if you need to create more value. You'll know if they're pleased with what you're telling them or can't wait till you quit. What you're going to look for are the following clues: the skin color of the person, skin tone, breathing, lower lip size, and pupils.

When you're speaking to a customer, note the color shifts that happen when you're giving them details. Did they have full color in their faces when you first saw them or was it all drained and pale? As a generalization, when the face is drained of color, they are not pleased with what you say and may feel uncomfortable or depressed, so change tactics and try again. They could be relaxed in your presence when the face is full of color. This is by no means the case for everyone, but in clusters, along with everything else you find, you must take this into account.

Skin tone (the tone of the muscles under the skin) should be noted. The facial muscles are either tight or they're nice and relaxed. This can be useful to see if a person feels uncomfortable or stressed by your company.

Your client's breathing is relevant because you want to know how to match it when we talk about the study. Usually, when someone is relaxed, their breathing will be slow and rhythmic. On the other hand, if a person feels anxious or threatened, then the breathing rate will become quicker to oxygenate the blood, and the color from the face will drain as the unconscious mind sends all the oxygenated blood to your legs and arms in unconscious anticipation of fight or flight. Be mindful of breathing and follow it in sync with other signals which you start picking up on.

Lower lip size again relates to whether or not they feel comfortable in your presence. If the lower lip is big and complete with no clear lines evident, this means it's full of blood and they're more definitely relaxed and like what you're doing. On the other hand, if the lower lip is thin and full of lines, it might mean the opposite, so be cautious. Remember, if your customer feels comfortable and happy, they will be more likely to be repeat customers and recommend you to other people.

Last but not least, let's look at the eyes; concentration and dilation. The eyes are fantastic, they're the only part of the brain we can see. We've all heard the phrase, "the eyes are the windows to the heart" and I'm not sure if that's true, but I know you can get a lot of information about what a customer is doing inside their heads, where their eyes are going, whether they're making images in their heads or hearing sounds, or whether they're having feelings.

If you're speaking to a customer and you note they've got really large and dilated pupils then it means they're either interested in what you're offering or they're interested in you! Ha-ha.

If the pupils are limited, on the other hand, it may be an indication that they were not interested in your idea at all. You must take lighting into account, of course, and this should be looked at just like everything else we've discussed.

Wandering eyes might mean they're imagining what you're telling them, or it might mean you've lost their attention and you're expected to do something to get them back on track. Focused eyes may mean that they're listening attentively to you.

Additionally, be mindful of the vocal tones and body posture of your clients.

- Is their voice strong and confident or sound threatening and unsure?
- Are they sitting or standing or are they free and relaxed with a closed body language?
- And how are you doing this?

Get out there and begin to notice people's shifts in posture. This will help you become a great communicator because you'll be able to judge whether your message gets through or doesn't let you change tactics and make sales.

More practice: this will make you a wizard in reading people. These are the skills Dr. Erickson taught in his mesmerizing act that we can apply to help us read people's body language as though we were reading their minds. But it doesn't stop there.

LEARN HOW BY USING YOUR MIND SKILLS

I see what you say

The idea here is that when we talk, the words we use in a conversation amount to around 40% of all the information that is transmitted. The rest is all contact that is not verbal. We may train ourselves to perceive and document minute information of other people we communicate with by using our perception and improving our perceptual acuity skills. We can learn how to see the facial tics, note the pauses, observe the movement of the ears, dilation of the pupils, shifts in the color of the skin, smiles, shrugs, micro-expressions that last for tenths of a second, among many other "tells" that most people are largely unaware they are giving us and that we seldom see. It seems like ESP or mind-reading is simply "reading" the non-verbal communication of somebody. The trick is to know how these signals can be elicited and analyzed to make them relevant to us.

Setting Up The Exercise

Use a standard deck of playing cards to create an exercise to enhance your perceptual acuity. By using cards in an inventive and playful setting, we can create an impersonal context or atmosphere in which micro-expressions can be elicited, detected, and used to 'divine' a target card. This will seem like 'mind reading'.

The mind reader's job is to try to find any signals that offer the card's identity when they apply to the deck's different attributes. The subject's job is not to disguise, foil or otherwise intentionally misdirect the reader's attempts to pick genuine face and body micro-expressions. They should aspire to be open and genuine. The subject aims to project a clear thought mentally, in this case, the card they have selected. There are no races or exams. It is essentially an exercise in skill-development similar to the application of scales on a piano.

Choose a card. Any card!

Allow the subject to hold the deck of cards face down. Pick a card. Hold the card toward the audience but do not look at it yourself. Make sure the audience gets a good look at it. Guide your subject to tell himself the ticket, silently. Encourage him to yell it to himself in silence. Inform him the card should be pictured vividly. They can keep their eyes closed, but in the back of their mind, they can still see the card. Let him extend it to a poster's size, or a museum painting, or even a billboard's size. Get him to blow it up, very good. Chant the card quietly, turn it into a cheer! Shout it, in his mind silently, and make the card's colors and details clearer, brighter. The intention here is to get that card's enhanced experience vividly in mind.

When they have the card's impression firmly in mind, start talking about the choices you can make about the selected card's attributes. Whether it's a red card or a black card, speak loudly. Be certain that when you say those distinguishing characteristics, they hear what you're saying and search for any betraying mark, move or gesture. For example, when you say, "It might be red or maybe it's black," they might look down or their pupils might dilate when you say the card matching attribute. Or they might pause for a beat longer in their breath or eye blink rate. Keep repeating the choice's variations until you feel you see an unconscious warning. Ask him specifically if your choice is right when you make your choice of which color it is. Was that a red card?

Then follow with other card attributes that are combined or opposed. A face card or a numbered card? Odd or even, king or queen? Whether it's a heart or diamond, clubs or spades, high number or low number. Don't just say "black or white." Turn it into an expression, make it part of a conversation, and be sure to look for those signs any time you mention both attributes and choose the one that seems to receive an implicit response. Declare your option and receive confirmation before progressing to the next set of choices.

If you're uncertain which of the opposite attributes will receive a response, continue to work until you get it. Keep the remaining card attributes limited until the goal card is the only remaining possibility.

The signals vary widely from person to person but the signals appear to be consistent once they have been identified for a given person. Don't tell them what their tell is if you want to proceed with this person in this exercise. If you tell them, failing to edit their replies, even if they do it unintentionally, will be impossible for them.

This method, as a scientific experiment, is quite flawed. But as an activity, it's fun to do and after you've done it, you'll learn a few things. If you're getting more than half of the cards right regularly, you're more effective than if by chance. Doing more of these activities will help to increase one's perceptual acuity, and increase one's confidence in communicating. Hypnotists, magicians, and NLP practitioners alike will build and use skills like these. Using these skills will make you look like a **mind reader**. Just like Dr. Erickson.

CHAPTER 2: PEOPLE-READERS ARE DEALMAKERS

Sales consultants should reach potential customers quickly. And this means we have to be able to read people and situations well to get that first connection right. Sadly, statistics tell us that 87% of women correctly interpret body language and circumstances, and only 42% of men are correct. However, if the consultant trains himself or herself to read people and adapt to what they see, the estimate may change dramatically.

One of the most valuable skills in sales today is the ability to read the body language of people, to know what to listen to in their voice, and then to know how to respond to what you hear. Get it right and connect with a potential client in the right way and they're going to feel relaxed. This is one of the ways you lead people to want to do business with you.

People all fall into one of four groups or tribes. Each tribe has a different interaction and decision-making style and different body language or hints. You'll find the ones closest to your style easiest to sell to. The opposite will be a real challenge to market to because perhaps the exact opposite of your social style and your approach to decision making. Here are the tribes. Which type are you?

THE LOGIC MAN

The man is the tribe of thought. He wants data he can read and think about before he makes a decision. He's not going to make a rash decision. He prefers going away and thinking things over with as much information as possible, and he's always going to have a strategy.

How do you see them?

You might feel that they are quite reserved and intense, and you might find it quite difficult to read them as they don't show a lot of body language. This group is the hardest to "read" of the four tribes.

Possible Issues

One of the issues with dealing with the Logic Person is that they can get bogged down with specifics and procrastinate to ensure accuracy when looking for all that data. They don't like changes or surprises, so they need to be well prepared for potential problems.

Estimates from the United States claim that 60% of males are in the Logic tribe. I don't have any figures for other nations, sadly, but you get the idea. And this proportion can be much higher if you are in an area with people working in the oil & gas industry.

THE ACTION MAN

This is the reverse of the theory, which is a problem for many contractors in building as they are people of action. Impatience is the secret to change. They hate huge quantities of information. They're fighting to fill out forms. They love challenges and are taking risks. They are determined, optimistic, and decisive.

How are you finding them?

Think speed-speaking, thinking fast, and moving fast. Give them some details and look at the glaze of their faces. But in making quick decisions, they're great.

Possible Problems

They may be somewhat frank or hostile as they tend to know when they are wrong. Which might mean that they're not listening well. They may also dominate somewhat.

THE FEELING INDIVIDUAL

The main concern of this tribe is how other people can affect their decisions. They are compassionate. They are easy-going and they are reliable.

How are you finding them?

They'll imagine how they'll feel about this home for their children. They will comment on what their family is going to love or hate. These are the warmest and friendliest men you can come across.

Possible Problems

They don't want to upset people because their worries or fears may not be clear. They're not going to argue, but they may not let you know they've changed their minds. They are not assertive people, and they can be very reactive. They can be put off by the direct action or friendly consultant with a casual comment off-the-cuff.

Also, figures from the United States suggest that 65% of the female population has a preference for the Feeling tribe.

THE FUN Man

Before they are seen, this man can often be heard. This person can find enthusiastic, creative, and ambitious room uses that you have not even considered. He may have some wild ideas for decoration as well.

How do you see them?

Not for nothing is this tribe named fun. They're going to be fun, imaginative, and dramatic at times. They can be very convincing and are so excited about new ideas. These are easy to 'read' and have quite dramatic body language at times. They're demanding and cheeky.

Possible Problems

This tribe easily bores. Some will skip through the show if they are with others and then become distracting while the others are just trying to look around. They can be distracted and undisciplined easily. Not good at finishing things.

Learn how to read your potential clients, activate their tribe, and make more sales, but more importantly, learn how to lead the opposite tribe to want to do business with you.

DO ASSOCIATIONS CREATE OUR PERCEPTIONS OF PEOPLE?

Many people have heard of the saying' do not judge a book by its cover,' and yet this is what happens so frequently. We see somebody wearing a certain clothing item, looking or behaving in a certain way, and making an instant decision.

This decision is an automatic and unconscious thought. And as a result of this cycle occurring so quickly, how one comes to such a conclusion is often unclear. These comparisons are going to be valid at times and sometimes they won't be.

Conditioning

Such connections are usually the result of one's earned conditioning. And the press is one of the most powerful forces in forming people's relationships. Family, friends, or romantic partners can also have a say in people's ego minds in the partnerships. And then there's the world of childhood. This is another incredibly important factor in which relationships you will come to have with others as an adult.

The Ego Mind

While this section is about the interactions you can have with people, this is how the ego mind works with everything. It doesn't need to be focused on what's true or functional; it can be dysfunctional and have no validity to it. But then the ego brain, depending on whether it is practical or inspiring, does not create such connections. Because it is familiar, it is created. This means that once something is marked as common, it is now known as what is secure. And now it is automatic instead of having to think about something and leads to less power being used. Thousands of years ago, when people lived in villages and were at risk of being eaten by animals, making snap judgments would not only save time, it would also save lives. And maybe this is when this ability came into being.

The Benefits

The Rewards: such comparisons make life easier when it comes to reading people and making snap judgments. If there was no such potential, it would lead to all sorts of issues. Finding something that usually takes seconds from wasting minutes and even hours. And instead of following the hints, one might even end up endangering their lives. This could be due to not being able to read the facial expression of a person or being unable to understand what might be harmful to someone carrying it.

The Halo Effect

There's something known as the halo effect where one identifies someone as having only one good characteristic as being a certain way based on it. This one characteristic contributes to the attribution of many other characteristics to them. It goes on automatically and without any conscious effort needing to be made.

A good example of this is when someone is found to be desirable to them. And because they are beautiful, they are typically associated as smart and even good. How beautiful someone is has little to do with how smart or effective they are. In reality, some people who are considered to be attractive will be smart and successful, and some will not.

This also works oppositely; if someone has a characteristic that is individually or socially perceived as negative, comparisons will be made. One may see another person taking drugs and could mark them out of this one trait to be dangerous and to have criminal tendencies.

And as the press likes to portray drug users in some way, the news will be the product of many of these interactions. People from all walks of life, though, are taking drugs and not everyone taking drugs is going to be risky or criminal.

Inaccurate Associations

Examples of incorrect comparisons are those above-mentioned. If one were to hire or date someone based on the first example or speak to or get to know someone from the second example and the assumptions proved to be wrong, it could lead to the creation of a new awareness.

Countries and Religions

Many relationships can be created around people from different countries or religions as a result of watching the news or reading the papers. They can also be incorrect and contribute to creating all sorts of challenges. This can result in violence, racism, and prejudice. Here, one does not see the individual on his own, but on the connections that were established through the press or social media, or propaganda. What they see are the stereotypes that are being placed onto others that the media has created in their minds.

The Younger Generation

Today's youth are often described as unruly, dangerous, and upsetting. For a few of the younger people, this may be the case, but it is not the entire truth. Nevertheless, one's mind can shape such connections by believing what the media says about the younger generation. Instead, keeping an open mind and seeing every situation for what it is can be difficult. Interpretations will be made unconsciously and this will make it difficult for people of all ages to see otherwise.

Men And Women

A person with a muscular physique may be viewed by men and women alike as violent or unapproachable, and yet this may be far from reality. For some exceptional cases, this will be valid, but it will not apply to all of them. It can be associated with attractive women as being vain and aloof. This can be wide of the mark. This will be the case for some women, but not all of them.

Absolute Meaning

The ego-mind works in absolutes, meaning all is either black or white. There's no middle ground with the brain, no gray area. And this means that the ego brain wants to either see these similarities or edit and refute anything that goes against them. Another thing that can happen is that the ego brain interprets truth in a way that matches these associations. And this may include projection use. This is completely protected by Anais Nin's statement "We don't see the world as it is, we see the world as we are." Read that again. It is a very powerful statement and may take some time to digest and process. It is worth contemplating more than once.

Awareness

The ego brain often perceives the present based on the past or a past combination. And that's why an understanding of how the ego mind works is critical. It has what is known as intuition, instincts, and hunches, and this may be another way to reach conclusions and make quick decisions. Associations promote life and save a great deal of time and resources. By being conscious of and challenging these connections, instead of being influenced through them, one will be able to have choices.

HOW TO READ A PERSON FROM THEIR PERSONAL HYGIENE

The first form of communication we send to people we meet is our presence. The person who sees you will have made some general assumptions about your character within the first five seconds based on how you look. Grooming naturally provides a wealth of information about who you are and what your personality could be. Hygiene will reveal the social appeal, laziness, intellect, social class, education, self-acceptance rate, culture, and organization of an individual.

You may be told by a lack of proper grooming that a person is lazy. They don't want to make an effort to clean themselves up and look presentable to everyone else, and this reflects on their ability to present other aspects of their lives, including their work ethics. It could be very bad. Be careful with this one because there are cultures out there for which this does not apply and you will have to understand the cultural background of the other individual.

Children growing up in poverty are typically not taught the basics of personal hygiene from experience in an American environment. It could be mental illness. There is a lack of proper hygiene among those who are stressed because they no longer have the energy or the desire to look presentable. Those with other persistent forms of mental illness such as depression, certain phobias, and Alzheimer's disease may also have poor hygiene, as they may not be able to understand the concept of proper hygiene. It could also be drug or alcohol misuse. People who abuse alcohol or drugs often have muddled complexions and a disheveled look. These same people are often suffering from depression.

It could be a medical problem. People who have suffered a traumatic injury or who have some kind of medical problem that restricts their mobility can lack proper hygiene.

It could be social ineptness. Someone who has a lack of proper hygiene going around in public may have a poor level of social intelligence. They live in their own world and can't have a good relationship with others or they don't know how others see them. Typically, these styles are interpersonal errors.

It could be self-centeredness. Someone who doesn't care about the impact the lack of hygiene has on both the people around them or about how others consider them shows a very stubborn, self-centered personality. They do what they want when they want, and how they want, irrespective of what others say.

Head-to-Bottom Hygiene Evaluation. When assessing a person, scan them from top to bottom and pay close attention to hygiene in doing so.

Hair / Scalp. Our hair is the primary characteristic of our body that we can alter and project our image into the world for others to see. That's why the army shaves their recruits' heads so they lose their sense of individuality and all look the same instead. Is their hair groomed? Is the skin clean or unwashed and greasy? Generally, dirty hair means the person is not showering.

Eyes. Face and eyes. For females, skin hygiene should be weighed more heavily because they place a high degree of importance on their faces. If it's a guy, how does he have his facial hair? Make-up or no make-up on a woman? How dry are his/her teeth? Do they have any teeth that are dirty or stained? Do they have broken teeth or teeth that are missing? Is she trimming her eyebrows? Does it look like they often wash their face? Are there overgrown hairs in the nose? Did they wash their eyes and nose from the junk?

Weight. Weight tells a lot about both the person's fitness level, out-look treatment, self-esteem level, and eating habits. There are very few people out there who are eager to wake up every morning to be bulging in the stomach. The real question is why they don't do anything about it.

Breath. Does their breath stink? This may be a symptom of not always brushing their teeth, having poor eating habits, suffering from anxiety, or having a medical condition.

Clothing. A good predictor of character is what we wear. Your clothes were dirty? Does their clothing have a bad scent? What is the state of the clothes they wear — beyond fashion trends?

Body Odor. Were they smelling of the body? If so, it may mean that they don't shower regularly or do not use deodorant. Beware of cultural differences where a strong body odor is appropriate.

Hands. Were they dirty in their hands? If so, why do they get dirty? Have they just been doing some research and lacked the care to wash their hands? Or perhaps they have a hobby which leaves their hands stained like a mechanic or a printer.

Nails of the hands. Are their fingernails clipped and kept? How filthy are their fingernails? Maintenance of the fingernail tells a lot about the attention to detail of the individual.

Identifying Coherence Standards: Any measure of poor grooming in itself should not speak for the person's character itself. A person you meet may have a logical reason to have dirty hands but seems clean in any other way. Maybe he's working as a mechanic. You want to look for several signs of a lack of hygiene, which is called. And do keep in mind cultural differences.

BODY LANGUAGE SPEAKS WITHOUT WORDS

Our non-verbal and body language is one of the most important forms of communication we use in our day-to-day experiences. It is the mode of communication that ignites the emotions and responses of our understanding. Studies have shown that having an understanding of body language improves one's potential to be effective in any given situation.

Have you ever looked at a couple sitting together and had a sense of how good or bad their relationship was in minutes? Have you ever noticed how easily, without any direct interaction, you were able to come to this conclusion? Whether you realize it or not, we spend our days listening to the non-verbal signals of people, interpreting their body language, and drawing conclusions about them.

The language of the body reveals the truth that we conceal from the world in words, including how we think about ourselves, our relationships, and our circumstances. The people we associate with can evaluate our motives, the nature of our relationships, how masterful we are in any given situation, our level of trust, and what our true motivations and interests are through our eye contact, movements, body position, and facial expressions.

The influence of body language is found in the emotional response it produces. In nearly every situation, emotions influence decisions and reactions. Non-verbal signals activate emotions that define an individual's core resources such as truthfulness, trustworthiness, honesty, skill level, and the ability to lead. The perception of these signals will decide who we are going to meet, the work we are hired for, our level of success, and who is elected into influential political positions.

Why aren't we spending years studying and improving successful body language skills? The truth is that most people underestimate the importance of body language before they try to gain an edge with a deeper understanding of human conduct in a personal relationship or a competitive business situation.

Open and Closed Presence Core Body Language Styles

Mastery in body language provides the keys for people to perceive the context behind particular body movements, as well as to provide an understanding of how to effectively convey and express messages while communicating with others. As a result, there is a substantial increase in the overall success of interpersonal relationships. Understanding the basics of the two core body language styles - open presence and closed presences - is the best way to start this mastery cycle.

Closed Presence

The closed presence body language style is found in individuals that fold their body around the centerline of the body, running straight from the top of the head to the feet down the middle of the body. The physical characteristics that generate this form of appearance are feet placed close to each other, arms held close to the body, hands crossed on the body and held together in front of the body, small hand movements kept close to the body, shoulders rolled in, and eyes focused below eye level.

The signals sent to the world by the body language form of closed presence are a lack of trust, low self-esteem, impotence, and lack of experience. In extreme cases, the message of wanting to be invisible can even be produced. The consequences of this type of body language on the person projecting may range from actually not receiving the best possible opportunities to a worst-case scenario of harboring a self-fulfilling perception of victimization.

Open Presence

The open presence, by comparison, is featured in individuals who create a sense of authority, energy, and leadership by projecting mastery of confidence, achievement, strength, and ability. The physical characteristic, open hand movements used in conversation away from the body's elbows, centerline holding away from the body, straight stance, shoulders held back, and eyes focused on their listeners' eye level. Such people are seen as beautiful, efficient, smart, and easily seeming to have achieved. We see this type of body language as the "leader's body language."

Eye contact aims to enhance the language of the body and to begin projecting an open presence. One of the most important communication methods we possess is eye contact. You can change the way people see you by using direct eye contact when communicating with others. Once people start speaking directly in the eyes of an individual, they are viewed as confident, trustworthy, and professional.

Hand gestures and facial expressions are the second level of transition with a transparent appearance that can be allowed to be seen. Both modes of communication improve the ability to clearly and effectively convey messages.

Through skillfully using open hands, and expressive facial features, greater impact is produced when speaking through engaging the audience more visually and increasing the amount of information provided during a conversation.

As children, we are taught from an early age that good boys and girls sit properly with legs and hands folded before them. The desire to limit physical space as children could establish some of the characteristics of the closed identity in adulthood found in body language. To combat this effect, one can start adopting the characteristics of the body language of the open presence and integrating these ways into their natural state of being. After completion of this behavioral change, it will provide the same non-verbal experiences and signals as their counterparts in the open environment.

To establish the most powerful presence in all interpersonal interactions, the mastery of body language is vital. Individuals without this knowledge are vulnerable to confusion and find their attempts inadequate in expressing their ideas. With the ability to differentiate between different body language styles, anyone can gain the mastery needed to succeed in whatever endeavor they want.

WOMEN'S BODY LANGUAGE

Body Language - the language of the key to reading your body, such as non-verbal movements, postures, and expressions, can certainly give you an advantage in the dating game. You talk much more non-verbally than verbally. Girls are more verbal and good at interpreting through body language.

There are two things to your use and concentrate on - observing the body language of people so when you see ten women in a bar you can tell which one is eager to meet you, and improving your body language signals to ensure that you are friendly, open and congruent, so your anatomy suits what you say.

Body language will help you get a good dating experience. Often only polite women do not initiate an approach - if there is no invitation then rejection is likely. Therefore, by finding out which people are open to approach, you can improve the odds. Learn how to read the body language of women so you know when you're in with a chance and can move on with trust, or when you're wasting your time and should cut down on your losses and run.

Is she in you interested?

Body language is used in two ways to improve your chances of success. First, you need to recognize which women are looking out for a person in a situation. Next, you must interpret the signals that are sent directly to you. Look around, check out the guys, scan the surroundings. If she is doing this and her eyes are resting on you, this is a sign that she is searching and is usable. Several key indicators may suggest that she is interested in you and any progress that you may make. Learning to read these signs is the key to improving your performance. She's staring at you, standing up, laughing, and grimacing. Learn how to read her as a book and then behave appropriately when you see a green light.

Watching and learning the language of the body is interesting. Knowing the cues and messages that your body sends out is one of the most important dating skills to learn.

Body language basics you need to think about. Messages from your body and your voice. Focus on her; look at her - her face, her attitude, her relation to you and others.

The above points apply to you as well. Be mindful of the signals that are sent out by every part of your body and posture. Your physiology is the main area to work on as you approach people. The rule of thumb is to keep eye contact, smile, and look polite. Eye contact can be considered aggressive, particularly if you have an unwavering stare. So just connect your eyes for a second or two longer than you usually do when you're finding out if a woman is interested. Without blinking, don't smile - she'll think you're a lunatic and don't frown - you'll look like you're in pain! When you receive a reply, act immediately.

If you want to get good with women, you'll have to make eye contact. Eye contact is one of the most powerful tools to communicate with someone else. Always interact with it. It is true the old saying 'the eyes are the windows to the soul.' People who are good at reading other people get a glimpse from their eyes of what is happening in their minds. And people who look at your face carefully sometimes make you feel like they're looking at you, not just your eyes.

A woman said that she once heard one of her male students say this was what she did to his friends. 'I was angry with her,' he said. 'It felt like she was able to see my thoughts!' Freaked out or not, she was fancied by that young man, and she thinks that moment of contact just fueled his attraction. Generally, it does.

Make eye contact as much as you can as you talk to her. The more she looks at you, the more curious she is. Most of us have a friendly eye, a positive voice that suits all circumstances in society. Under the mask, you're searching for the gestures. Her true feelings will flash up and will cross her face every so often. It's like we can't hold the mask ALL the time in place. It's falling.

In western cultures, direct eye contact is generally expected. It shows you're interested in the person you're talking to and what you have to say. It builds confidence and strengthens the bond with the person with whom you interact. We generally keep eye contact for about one-third of the time when we talk to someone, looking away from time to time. It indicates you're lonely or have something to hide to look at someone less. It may express a lack of interest or discomfort with the speaker. We may be irritated by staring at someone for longer periods and, conversely, show enthusiasm and concern. This depends on what follows the prolonged eye contact with other non-verbal communication.

It takes practice to do this to read someone's expressions. Practice a female friend, daughter, or mother with whom you get along well. Get into the habit of looking at their faces and try to catch the momentary changes to gain insight into what they feel or think. Ask them if you start picking up something. 'You were irritated,' you might say. If they're willing to play this guessing game with you, they're going to tell you what they think at that moment. They may not even have known their discomfort showed in their eyes. It's going to be a bit of a shock for them to say they felt it.

On the web, there are some quizzes of facial expression worth trying out. But if you're not doing well, don't be too upset. I'm pretty good at reading people, but I've misread many of their examples. It's not an exact study, so don't expect it to be flawless. But if you can get into the ballpark somewhere and use the input process of asking to see if you're wrong, you'll get better at it, and you'll get better with girls as well. It's like interpreting a mathematical equation or computer program to learn how to interpret facial expressions. You can do that. All you have to do is learn the rules. Note, I didn't say anything about what she's talking about? That's because any interaction is the least important part of it. Learn to read her face and other non-verbal clues and know whether you succeed or fall flat on your face without having to hear her say a word.

Reading eyes works in both directions - your eyes represent your innermost thoughts; their eyes show how they feel. You interact more with your eyes than any other part of your body - you can't flirt without communicating with your face.

Other Parts of the Body

Give powerful messages to your hands. Are they in our pockets or waving wildly about, open or closed, apart or touching? The movements of an open hand show openness, honesty, and friendliness.

Your posture will convey a wide range of messages to anyone interested in looking. If you feel defensive or vulnerable, and whether you want to be there, it can show your involvement or otherwise. In your search for a date, all these are important signals given to you.

Her Body Language: When trying to read her body language, the most important point to remember is that you can't determine what she's thinking by just seeing one indication of body language. You need to check for indicators of behavior classes. Folded arms can mean that she puts up a barrier. Instead, she may be freezing, she's spilled something down her blouse and she's trying to cover it up, or it's just the way she's always sitting down. However, it's not how she looks that's significant, but more often it's the most telling shift in body language. When she goes from leaning forward, looking into your eyes and smiling back to leaning back, folding her hands, frowning, and avoiding eye contact then she's changed her mood and it's up to you to understand why and respond.

Handshakes, arms, and feet. One of the first things you do when you meet someone is to shake hands. What do you mean by your handshake? What are the handshakes of others revealing about them? I'm still shocked when I shake hands with someone who's offering their fingers and treating them as a limp shrimp. It's just as upsetting to get your hand grabbed by someone who seems to be trying to break your hand. Not too strong. Not too frail. Your handshake says a lot about you and you need to make it perfect.

Hands are not for shaking alone. It implies authenticity and truthfulness to reveal them as you act. Movements downward with your hands suggest authority. An individual may make a fist and gesture to mean 'at a boy'. For emphasis, one may pound their fist on a table. Clenching one's hands implies hostility and rage.

Talking with one's hands shows openness and engagement, particularly with exposed palms.

Leaning forward or backward. Lean toward people who are interested. We normally condemn people or stay aloof when someone leans backward.

Standing and distance from each other. Many people in the U.S. are relaxed just under two feet away from someone they're talking to. When further apart, there is discomfort. Closer has sexual overtones and generates reactions in line with one's approaching feelings. Comfortable distances, like other nonverbal signals, vary dramatically from culture to culture.

Nodding. In response to the remarks of another, nodding shows curiosity and understanding. Bobbing one's head, on the other hand, indicates you are tuned out by the person you're talking to. Head shaking is typically a negative response.

Smiles. Smiles show interest, anticipation, passion, compassion, and a variety of other positive reactions. To express a positive response, there is nothing like a genuine smile. On the other hand, frowning or lip narrowing is negative.

Expressions of the eyes. One may be perplexed by a wrinkled forehead. Elevated eyebrows may indicate enlightenment. Seen all the time suggests a lack of confidence.

Frequently opening one's mouth makes it seem like you want to interrupt. Try to look at others and their facial expressions to see all the things that can be communicated.

Inspiration. In some cultures, using movements to communicate is more common than in others. On the other hand, fidgeting is most often a sign of fatigue, nervousness, and caution. Be cautious with touching. It is quick to misconstrue a well-intentioned touch. Be vigilant. The actual touch demonstrates attraction. In a dating situation, if a woman starts touching another male, however innocently, she shows interest in them. Avoid touching improperly. Inappropriate touching in the workplace is nothing more than a hug. Do touch in relationships between people. You may feel strained, but that embrace will be enjoyed by your partner.

Watch out for the person you're talking to. Where are they standing and sitting in? How quickly do they speak? What's their breathing rate. Try to imitate these signals to establish a relationship faster.

Note to make. Would you like to let the person you're talking to know you're going to find out what they're saying? Please take notes. It's a great compliment.

Stay congruent with your verbal and non-verbal messages. This is the best way to get your messages through. Furthermore, when, in a friendly voice, you make a hostile remark, the listener will dismiss the animosity and view the message as friendly. And that's because non-verbal contact is better than the words you're saying.

COMMON NON-VERBAL MISTAKES

Our body is our most valuable asset, allowing us to do everything from building houses from the ground up to the taste of a fine wine's most subtle flavors. For everything, our body has complex systems; breathing, feeding, speaking, even talking. What most people fail to realize is that our bodies are constantly showing clear signs of what is happening to our minds. These can be good, to say the least, for our contact.

Some of us, especially women, are interested in subtle signs in body language. But some aren't. Some may interpret the signs better than others (maybe through self-training or just plain experience), which usually means they can transmit the same signs easily as well. This seems almost unfair to someone who is not as aware of their non-verbal signal. Read the following for those of you who understand the value of non-verbal communication or want to gain a better handle on their social life.

These are some of the most common non-verbal "errors."

- *Shifty Eye Contact* - This is one of the most common mistakes I see today, it's also one of the most IMPORTANT things to be managed. Eye contact is a huge asset to have under your command, it can tell someone that you are secure in your interaction (and your skin), while it can also show people that you are someone that can be taken seriously. Shifty eye contact can make you look like you're not comfortable, you're insecure, socially awkward, inexperienced, or have a lack of self-confidence (which ultimately causes a lack of confidence from others) and the list goes on.

If two lions face each other, they must look each other in the eyes. They measure the "power" of the other and decide their position. The alpha is confirmed by the best eye contact while the shifty, soft eye contact confirms the beta. Nevertheless, this often means death or exile for a lion. Death or exile normally won't happen in our human world. But that doesn't mean shifty eye contact doesn't matter. Strong eye contact means strong character, someone who believes in their values, and someone who is not afraid of who they are.

Effective Approach - Take note of your eye contact with others from this moment on. See how some people change it. Take note of the modifications. Focus in conversation on your eye contact. Keep a lot of eye contact, but it's not a competition of stares. At first, it may seem like knives shooting from eye contact into your eyes; it's going to go away. You may also make eye contact so much that it is odd and uncomfortable. That will also subside; you will finally have a relaxed, normal connection with your eyes. Remember how the reactions of other people change over time.

- *Closed Body Language* - Whether you are a man or a woman, your body language can give similar signals (depending on the type of contact in which you are participating). Closed language of the body is a great indicator of a lack of social skills. *Note*: you are inaccessible to those around you. You're not open to change or new experiences. You may be, but your body will say otherwise. A person in a conversation that is closed to you might look a little odd, almost anti-social. They might like they're hiding from you, or maybe even scared of you, or more specifically, scared of what you might think. It goes both ways. What does the language of your body say? Clear body language indicates that someone is lacking in terror, that they are not afraid or ashamed to express themselves. The language of the open body is often viewed as welcoming, and also makes contact with the other more relaxed person. Closed as opposed to open. What does your body say? Closed arms are a sure sign of closed body language as arms can be opened freely on your sides or hips. Hands in pockets that are locked vs. hands that are free from pockets. Get it? Get it?

Effective approach - Try opening up the next time you're in a conversation. If your body language is shut, opening up can feel like revealing yourself, at first, perhaps leaving you vulnerable. Relax. There's no risk that a spear will be fired at your head. Relax. Open up, and see the reaction difference.

- *Nervous jitters* - Does anyone ever see weight move from one foot to another? Or maybe (a lot of times) pick their fingernails? Scratch the eyes, scratch the nose, jiggle the keys in the hands or pockets? The list continues. These are all nervous jitters cases. Some are MOST obvious, and some are less apparent. You can usually tell when someone is anxious. You can imagine why somebody is doing this. "Why are you so anxious?"

Nervous jitters tell you a lot of negative things, even to your advantage. Take a nervous jitters mental note and start working it out in your mind. If you have a jiggling key problem, you might want to hold it out of your pockets. Eliminating it is easy once you can identify them.

Effective approach - Take your anxious jitters mental note. Also, you'll interact with the absence of anxious jitters from now on. It may take a while. Hold on. You'll soon find out it's not that nerve-wracking.

There are many more non-verbal "errors" but try to take note of your personal "errors" for now. Are you any of the above? If so, focus on the exercises I mentioned above for the active approach and see them trickle back one by one. In my experience, these are the greatest breakers of social interactions. It refers in general to corporate and technical contact. Employers look at these during interviews, as well as a number during dating. Remember your customs.

CHAPTER 3: BUILDING YOUR LISTENING SKILLS

We also connect by email in our world today. This is a verbal and non-vocal form of communication. In other words, to communicate with each other, we use written words, but not our voice.

Communication is verbal or emotional when speaking to someone on the phone. Hearing the voice of someone is an added aspect of interaction and is often considered more important and easier to understand.

We experience verbal and vocal interaction when we meet someone in person, and we have the added advantage of non-verbal and non-vocal communication. It ensures that we can track the expressions and movements on their faces. We can also see the orientation of their body, their stance, how they move in their personal space, whether or not they make eye contact, and even their appearance. Such non-verbal/non-vocal findings can give us a huge amount of information. That is as long as non-verbal/non-vocal interaction is compatible with vocal/verbal communication.

Imagine an excited person saying, "I'm happy to be here" with a big smile on his face, rapidly and loudly. He uses his non-verbal/non-vocal signals to convey what he thinks, what he wants, what his desires are. We emphasize the verbal/vocal message as well as the non-verbal/vocal interaction because it includes the intonation used by the person speaking, the sound of the voice, the rhythm, the rate at which they are speaking, and even if they are pausing or sighing. Generally, this is the way people interact.

Then imagine a person with a poor posture saying, "I'm so glad to be here," eyes down, and quiet, unenthusiastic voice. He also says, "I'm so glad to be here," but this leads to confusion as there is a difference between his vocal/non-verbal message and his vocal/verbal response. Individuals don't always say what they mean or mean what they say, so it's not always easy to know what a person feels for sure. Communication can be very complex, as you can see, including written words, spoken words, facial expressions and movements, and sound, pitch, and speed and tone. Start tuning and improving your listening skills by listening to verbal, non-verbal, auditory, and non-vocal communication with your ears and eyes.

HOW TO DISCOVER CONFIDENCE

We must have felt confident at some times. Even when we need it, it's a bit hard to regain faith. There are simple activities that can be done to get your confidence back on track as soon as you need it. There are seven ways to be confident: first-watch your attitude - this may not sound like a partnership with the confidence we're talking about, but the way you're sitting or standing can send messages to people around you. If that message expresses trust, you will receive a positive response from others, which will, of course, raise your confidence. So start watching your sitting and standing to prove your confidence.

The second way - associate with people with confidence and positive thinking. Neighborhood has an enormous impact on others. When you tend to associate with low-confidence men, complainants, and pessimists, no matter how much esteem you have, it will slowly but surely disappear and be pulled to suit your neighborhood. When, on the other hand, you are surrounded by people full of happiness and trust, it will also create a positive environment that will bring benefits to you.

The third way is a feeling of confidence, and if you ever feel it once, it is not impossible to feel it again. Remembering the moment when you felt confident and in control can make you feel and help put a sense of confidence in your mind.

The fourth approach – exercise. The trick is to exercise as often as possible whenever you want to feel confident. You won't have trouble displaying confidence whenever necessary with a qualified skill.

The fifth way - Know yourself. Think about yourself and all the things you know you can do well. If you're having trouble doing this, note people's feedback. What do people say you are doing well? Writing all of this down is a good idea until you can see it again to boost self-confidence anytime inspiration is needed. I keep a file of every positive email I receive from a client. It's a good reference for when I need to send something to a new client as well as a reminder to myself when I need a confidence boost.

The sixth way - don't be too harsh on yourself. Don't be dismissive of yourself; you've got to be your best friend.

But when a friend is going through a difficult situation, you won't want to get involved in the problem, cause it's going to emotionally drain you, right? You don't want it, of course. Positive talk can turn into the best weapon for improving self-confidence, so make sure you set the habit, don't let others' problems get you down.

The seventh way - Don't be afraid to take a chance if you're a risk-taker. You'll find this action will build trust in yourself. However, this also works well to reduce your anxiety about things you don't know, plus it can boost confidence considerably.

THE COMMUNICATING CONFIDENCE GUIDE

Strong-minded people have faith in themselves and can express that sense of trust to others even when they may not feel particularly confident. What separates them from shy people is their body language, and it is this posture that is essential to send the right message or signal to others. This aura of faith that is immediately released is crucial in all areas of life from business negotiations to attracting other people. The more relaxed you are, the more confident you are, and the more confidence people have in you. Confident people have that 'something' about them that makes things turn to their favor, and they always seem to have the lucky breaks in life.

What other people do not realize is that achieving this highly desirable value is not too difficult. The key to being a confident person is to act honestly before others even though you may have your own personal and private issues inside. Bluffing with a poor poker hand and playing on stage are perfect examples of how much more relaxed you are behaving and the more people believe they see you as the real deal.

Habits are another field that separates confident people from shy people. Empowering habits will improve your life to no-end, and as a result, you will boost your faith by developing the right habits for thinking and communicating. With your newly found faith in your ability, the change in your life will leave you ecstatic.

Confidence can be expressed through positive thinking. By displaying a much more positive disposition, practicing your confidence through remembering memories or interactions of trust from your past will show this in your physiology. At the same time, the higher your level of physical confidence, the more confident your psychological reasoning will be. Note, as a single entity, the body and mind still work together in tandem.

Extra trust can be gained by looking at how people behave with confidence. Research their self-confident walk and gestures, consider their body posture and wonder about their thoughts. You can create an identity for the' ideal' individual by doing this. Take your ideal person's identity and make use of the features you have witnessed. Ignore the negative body language cues that some people give out to exude distrust. Slouching, avoiding eye contact, or hanging one's head are actions that you should avoid as they show a lack of self-control and submissiveness. This also refers to angry or panicky behavior, which means that you are not in control of the situation. Throughout stress situations, optimistic people are cool and relaxed and are usually chosen as leaders as they have the right qualities to solve any problems. Therefore, you have to try to adopt the qualities of a leader to meet those of a positive one.

Instead of pointing fingers, gesturing, or accusing others, people who are fully confident tend to seek solutions to any problems they face while showing a positive attitude towards the outside. Trust is correlated with intensity, which explains why it attracts others. Imagine going to a job interview trying to sell yourself and not having much faith in yourself. If you do not believe in yourself, how can a potential employer believe in you? You will ultimately become a much more confident person simply by acting confidently.

WHEN YOU ARE BETRAYED BY BODY LANGUAGE

If you've read anything about body language, you're likely to hear that 90% of interaction is non-verbal. The real source of this slightly distorted statistic, which concluded in the 1971 study 'Silent Messages' is that interaction in each conversation is 7% letters, 38% voice sounds and 55% facial expression. Consequently, body language is born in 90% (or rather 93%) of all contact. Nonetheless, believing that most contact is made by body language would be incorrect. We typically don't contradict what people say in everyday life, so what is fascinating about body language and how helpful body language is concerned with what is being said.

In people with advanced dementia, physical appearance is an important factor in pain assessment due to the decreased ability to communicate verbally, but in almost all situations, a nurse would not rely on how a patient behaves to determine how much pain a person has. They would ask the patient. Similarly, if someone sits with their arms and legs crossed and looks annoyed on their face, you probably won't be talking to them. Body language is 100% of contact in this situation, but the only way to make sure is to talk to them. Through revealing your emotions and mood, body language betrays you, yet it is your words and their interaction with your body language that is central to your communication.

Notwithstanding the essentials of body language in interaction, non-verbal communication is quite limited without a verbal component of communication. It's the combination of words and body language that betrays you, especially when you don't suit what you say with how you behave. Mehrabian defined congruence or continuity between body language and words as a crucial element of non-verbal communication study; finding when the words and actions of an individual fit or fail to match.

But surely you have nothing to worry about if a person hasn't learned body language? Until body language books existed, people picked up on the signals without being fully aware of what they were picking up on. You won't need a book on body language to help you read the signs when someone says they're happy but don't look happy. Even if the person you spoke to didn't read the books, their body language is highly likely to betray them.

When you deal with other people daily, what you need to be concerned with is not what you say, but how you behave in response to what you say. If you're saying enthusiastic things, your body language can be all chaotic and excited, but when you're lying, the situation is different. But if you tell the truth, why do you want the language of the body to be fake? The response is that we're only human. Sometimes when we tell our partners nice things or talk to our bosses, we're just too lazy or just not involved. We can talk about the one thing we think is the world's most interesting or exciting thing, but if we're hungry, or exhausted, or sick, or just having a bad day, the words we use may be excited, but our body language may betray us. How are you falsifying it? Many experts say that you can't manipulate the language of your body.

If you've read 'top ten signs she likes you' or 'how to tell if he's cheating', this is good news. But if you're trying to make yourself look good for the boss then it might be an issue.

So, what are we going to do? The simple answer is to increase the difference between what we say and the language of our body. We are growing incongruence in two ways: the first thing we can do is to be frank. If you're not, do not try to sound too excited. Do not try to compensate if you feel tired by being overly excited. You may be excited about it but do it not overcompensate. Don't lie if you disagree with someone. Only stop responding directly to them as much as possible. So when your friend or girlfriend asks "Do I look fat in this?" Don't respond with "you look great" or "you look good in that dress" and then try to change the subject. You're probably lying, whether you say yes or no. Therefore, don't answer the question. Don't avoid the topic, but don't answer the question directly.

The second thing we can do is learn how to think and do something else. Congruence is about consistency; you should be able to make interpreting them hard and thus break congruence when you cast doubt on the continuity of the symbols. Although telling the truth can be a delicate matter, disturbing your body language's congruence would allow you to think about how you feel and learn something about body language. It doesn't require a lot of details, but you should be mindful that body language is usually considered to function in clusters, so what you're doing with your arms is only important when it's about your face's expression and how you're standing. You will want to break down the clusters of your acts and potentially interrupt congruence when you need to make sure that someone doesn't read anything about you from the rest of your body language.

Body language areas to concentrate on:

Facial expressions: if you're feeling bored then you're showing interest, if you're comfortable showing a little disappointment, if you don't have something to say, make it look like you want to tell. If anyone you talk to offers you the opportunity to speak and you don't, they're going to start challenging their perception of you.

Eye contact: failure to maintain contact with the eyes indicates a lack of interest or frustration. Aggressively sustained eye contact indicates another person's desire to conquer. Measure your thoughts and desires and change contact with your eyes accordingly.

Arms and legs: all kinds of things about you are revealed by your stance. Two things to be mindful of are arms and legs pointing and body posture open or closed. We also show interest in someone by pointing to them with our arms and legs. If we're not interested or eager to go, we could point our limbs to the door in an attempt to be ready when it's time to go. The distinction between crossed arms and legs and uncrossed arms and legs is the open or closed body pose on a very basic level. "I'm not interested or listening," says the closed body. An open body says the opposite.

Voice tone: how are you behaving normally? Are you a fast loudspeaker, a very quiet speaker? When you're mad, think about how you sound. Don't get taken away too much. If you're just tired, you don't want the boss to feel you're violent, so think about size, pace, tone, and infuse a little emotion with your speech.

The language of your body will deceive you. The uncontrollable incongruity between how you behave and what you say will say something you don't want it to. Talk about what you'd like to do and how you think, and then do something completely different. A minor noise goes a long way.

Disrupting the language of the body can be hard work and you wouldn't want to do anything all the time. If you use it on an exceptionally perceptive buddy regularly, they will pick up your cues and see your plan through. You can fight back against the deceit of body language when you interrupt congruence if you feel uncertain.

What body language is

Brain science Today clarifies that body language includes the way that humans send an implicit sign to each other. Stance, hand signals, and even the most diminutive outward appearances are unwittingly translated by people who probably won't know that they are seeing them. Body language conveys immediately and easily a person's solace or inconvenience in a given circumstance. A person's outward appearance or position can alarm others to peril. For example, suppose someone opens a cooler and takes a drink of soured milk. A wound articulation and eyes wide with alert quickly send the message, "disregard this!" in this way saving others the sorry experience of drinking the milk for themselves. An old piece of the mind called the limbic cerebrum is for the most part in charge of communicating implicit sentiments utilizing motion, facial changes, and wild eye-widening. Miniaturized scale articulations are short-lived and pass on obvious feelings even in grown-ups who can, for the most part, control their outward appearances somewhat.

What body language isn't

Body language, just as the craft of reading people, isn't a definite science. There are no rigid standards when it comes to deciphering the implicit expectations of another person. Indeed, even researchers who were prepared to secure the ability to read people like a book commit errors, particularly when watching a person who is talented at controlling a lot of their cognizant physical conduct.

Instructions to read a person like a book

Some human sign is naturally comprehended. Imagine you watch out your window and see a bystander hustling along the walkway, leaning forward with his arms folded over himself. Your underlying response would, without a doubt be, "it's cold and blustery outside."

In a one-on-one discussion, a person with their arms crossed sends an implicit sign that they are shielding their personal space. That person may, in any case, essentially be worn out or cold.

Mind specialists clarify that feelings occur before the musings. The time range between is simple nanoseconds, however, that is long enough for a perceptive human to sense the appetite, outrage, impatience, or joy of another person momentarily. Humans are specialists at rapidly making sense of another person's demeanor, and they do it before a solitary sentence is spoken. People instinctually look when experiencing another human. Humans unknowingly look at breathing rate, stance, and articulation. Although a few grown-ups have figured out how to by and large control fundamental facial expressions, the eyes uncover much. When a person investigates the eyes of someone they appreciate, their pupils may enlarge. Moreover, when they see an item that they want. The second (and third) thing a great many people see about another person is their hands. Open palms and clenched hands may state everything one has to know in a moment.

The most effective method to utilize body language to your advantage

We've all done it at one time or another. You're sitting with your dear old aunt, and the discussion is exhausting you senseless. You cherish her and would prefer not to offend her, so you grin and gesture as your aunt drifts endlessly on and on. You lean toward her, look in her eyes, and touch her hand. These are cognizant signs that pass on family relationships. When it's time to go, you check the time and turn your toes toward the exit. This sends an unpretentious sign that the visit, however important, is coming to an amicable close.

Body language passes on a first – and second and third – impact on anybody and everybody you meet. To establish a positive connection, grin when you meet someone. Focus on your stance and stand or sit straight and still. Shifting load from foot to foot shows pressure and uneasiness. Try not to squirm, and do make certain to keep in touch as you shake someone's hand.

Body language wouldn't fret reading, nor does it give knowledge into what another person is thinking. When reading people cautiously, body language causes you to comprehend another person's obvious aim. Nonetheless, you can develop empathy as you grow; it doesn't continue as before. Furthermore, for the individuals who feel they need empathy or know someone who appears to be cold or inaccessible, there are ways they can figure out how to be progressively sympathetic.

Science says we can develop empathy.

Neuroscientists found a territory in the mind, which if ever damaged, can influence the capacity to perceive empathy. Besides this, we are prepared to be social creatures, yet to different degrees. The majority of the relationship aptitudes are developed at an early age, yet the capacity to feel for others can grow all during one's life.

This implies we can develop empathy from numerous points of view. Look at these.

- Reading books

While reading books of various types can help develop empathy, reading fiction appears to have the most significant impact. The capacity to find out about things outside our own reality encourages us to assemble an association with others too. If we can feel for a desolate mythical serpent or a talking pig, we can most likely associate this way with people in actual circumstances. Maybe these accounts prepare our feelings so we can be there for others.

- Practice Patience

While being patient isn't always a simple assignment, it can prompt winding up progressively more compassionate to your man. Patience causes us to stop amidst unrest and envision how other people must feel experiencing comparable circumstances. If you're furious with someone, before lashing out, take a couple of snapshots of patient review and find the reality behind these irate feelings. Patience permits you time to regroup and instructs you to develop an astounding measure of empathy.

- Care

Another way to develop affectability and empathy is through care. Monitoring every single physical sensation and taking deep breaths keeps us grounded. Contemplation is a piece of care and can help focus the brain on the present, hence enabling us to feel further sensations and associate with others the unadulterated structure.

As we figure out how to process calm or self-empathy, we will grow more noteworthy capacities to sympathize with the agony of others. It resembles figuring out how to step into someone else's perspective.

- Learning Another Language

Being bilingual can likewise enable you to figure out how to be increasingly sympathetic. This is particularly valid for little kids learning various languages, perhaps because of relatives of different societies. As youngsters learn, they should understand which language is being utilized, and understand rapidly.

This enables them to learn, words, yet different feelings communicated differently from culture to culture. This can extraordinarily develop a high sense of empathy from the beginning.

- Unity/otherworldliness

To be genuinely sympathetic, you should truly think about others. The individuals who practice otherworldliness or something similar, do, for the most part, care about the lives of others, even to the point of giving things and making a special effort to help in bigger ways.

One thought of otherworldliness is unity.

- Imagination

Imagination is a demonstration of creating new thoughts that are reasonable to the fitting state of life

We're not static animals. You can always improve, in character and numerous other ways. You can develop a sense of empathy where you had none previously. We are human, and we, as a whole, have feelings. Regardless of whether they've been pushed down from past injuries, solidified by offensive conditions, or just showed restricting perspectives.

Having the option to feel for others is significant. Don't you need someone to identify with what you're sometimes feeling? It doesn't take heaps of quick work to develop empathy, and it just takes consistency and patience.

After some time, you will have changed so much, and you won't have the option to perceive that old hard heart any longer. A delicate beefy one will have supplanted it…a heart that feels and thinks about the life and love of individual human creatures.

Some things introverted people do sound good to them yet not to every other person. Also, more often than not, these things have to do with the way an introvert's mind works. We don't attempt to stick out or get consideration by carrying on unpredictably – we need to remain agreeable in a comfortable introverted shell.

Here are some behaviors any introvert will engage in and the little-known explanations for them:

Not receiving phone calls and pretending they are not at home

Truly, most introverts abstain from talking on the phone or if nothing else incline towards a different kind of communication. The sound of a ringing mobile or doorbell can be genuinely terrifying when you don't anticipate any calls or guests. What's more, it has to do with the idea of individual space which is hallowed for all introverts. Getting a call from a stranger or seeing an unforeseen guest at their entryway resembles somebody attacking your mystery sanctuary of calm and isolation. Maybe somebody is compromising the ideal amicability of quietness and protection that you made. Furthermore, any introvert will effectively secure their hallowed private space so that they will maintain a strategic distance from these types of situations at any expense.

Introverts likewise need time to break down a situation and thoroughly consider it to concoct the best answer. That is why they incline toward composed communication over talking. It gives them the essential time to think and express contemplations in an ideal way. A phone call doesn't give us this benefit.

Abstaining from making phone calls

The case where you have to make a phone call can be all the more terrifying for an introvert. Sometimes it can take 20 minutes or so to find the courage, set up your considerations, and dial that phone number. Why do introverts battle with making phone calls so much? By and large, introverts don't care for unexpected results. That is why they feel awkward with calling outsiders or people they don't know well. No one can tell where that phone discussion is going to head, isn't that right?

Introverts likewise will, in general, depend on non-verbal communication, which incorporates non-verbal communication, outward appearances, and other behavioral subtleties. They are, indeed, quite good at understanding people and identifying little irregularities in their behaviors, which uncover inauthenticity and untruths. So it makes sense why not seeing the individual we are talking to doesn't help by any stretch of the imagination. An introvert will feel as though a significant segment of communication is absent.

Escaping neighbors or colleagues in the road

Let's face it with one another. What number of you, as individual introverts, have acted extremely weird at seeing a partner or an old classmate cruising by? You may have taken cover behind a market rack or hidden your face, imagining you are hacking. Also, before venturing out from home, you may have checked through the peephole and the blinds to make sure neighbors are not there. Why does going over a colleague make introverts that awkward? The appropriate response is basic – we don't care for constrained discussions. Introverts acknowledge important communication with similarly invested people they can trust. So having well-disposed gab pressed with casual conversation themes and ungainly questions isn't the thing by any means. Introverts need to talk when they truly have a remark, not because the unwritten social principles expect them to. That is why we fear running into a classmate who may pose us awkward individual inquiries or a well-disposed old neighbor who is consistently up to casual chitchat.

Utilizing extreme resistance components

A portion of the manners in which an introvert protects themselves from the external world may include some unusual behaviors. A few examples incorporate wearing headphones when we are not tuning in to music or stowing away in the washroom. This shields us from the superfluous social association. For example, if you need to approach somebody for directions, you will be more reluctant to deliver your inquiry to an individual who is wearing headphones, isn't that so? Introverts realize that, so it's essentially one of the methods for ensuring their sacrosanct individual shell is not disrupted.

To the washroom - introverts use it as a shelter while grinding away or at a party. Not just talking yet even simply being around other people for a long time can be profoundly depleting for us. So we have to take a break to revive our vitality levels. That is why putting in time in the washroom allows us to confine ourselves from the outer world and consequently recapture the vitality for the time being.

Claiming to have designs however actually simply remaining at home

Another one of the behaviors introverts are known for is dismissing an invitation, saying you have plans. In actuality, however, you remain at home without anyone else's input to watch a movie, accomplish something inventive or read a book. Each introvert acknowledges sooner or later in their lives that it's simpler to state they have plans with other people than to clarify why they have a ton of fun alone at home rather than at some get-together. This has an immediate association with how an introvert's mind works.

It depends on a synapse called acetylcholine while an outgoing person's mind depends on dopamine. Dopamine takes part in crafting the mind's pleasure and reward focuses. It essentially makes us notice and pursue outside remunerations, for example, social communication, dynamic games, or undertakings. This implies since introverts don't depend on a dopamine discharge, they find social association less remunerating than outgoing people.

Hence, an introvert finds calm single exercises all the more fulfilling, for example, a stroll in the recreation center or perusing a book. This clarifies why we frequently favor remaining at home to heading off to a gathering – we mostly realize that we will have a good time more along these lines.

Unusual introvert behaviors make perfect sense…to introverts

As you see, each one of those weird behaviors has flawlessly coherent explanations for them, and each introvert realizes that. Presently, the test is to disclose them to their outgoing relatives and companions. Be that as it may, trust me, with time, they will comprehend and value your introverted character.

CHAPTER 4: HOW BODY LANGUAGE IMPROVES YOUR MINDSET

Our body language is the way we speak with our outside world – and the more significant part of us doesn't understand we are doing it! Body language phenomenally affects the center of who you are as an individual. It impacts our posture and physiological wellbeing, yet it can change our psychological viewpoint, our impression of the world, and others' perception of us.

HOW OUR BODY SPEAKS

We utilize our body language to communicate our musings, thoughts, feelings. We synchronize body movements to the words that we express. We impart purposefully through activities like shrugging our shoulders or applauding just as through inadvertent actions like collapsing in on ourselves or pointing our feet an alternate way toward the individual we are speaking with. Before spoken language was made, our body language was the primary technique for communicating. Our body is our major method to express ourselves within our lives!

How can it influence our state of mind?

Our body language is the way that we interface with the outside world and it is also the way that we associate with ourselves. How do you treat yourself? Do you slouch over when you walk, or do you walk tall and proud? It is true to say that you are thankful for each development that your body makes for you? Most likely not. We regularly underestimate our bodies. We frequently decide to condemn it. Or take it for granted.

Body language can impact our physical body and posture. However, it can change how we are feeling. Having a great attitude can affect misery and causes us to keep up elevated levels of confidence and energy when we are confronted with pressure. Having great posture, positive body language, can also change our attitude so that we can reach that positive feeling, increase our confidence, project energy, and a winning outlook.

An up-and-coming field of psychology, known as the mind-body-connection, asserts that the association between our body and our general surroundings doesn't merely impact us. We are personally woven into the way that we think. Studies in this field show that the individuals who are sitting in a hard seat are less inclined to bargain than those sitting in a delicate chair, and those holding warm beverages saw others as more mindful and liberal than those holding cold drinks. This examination shows that body language is a two-way road prompting both the outside and inner world.

FOUR DIFFERENT WAYS YOU CAN CHANGE YOUR BODY LANGUAGE

The followings are four ways you can change your body language.

Flip around that glare!

Grinning and laughing are infectious! A complete report on smiling found that a grin that draws in the mouth and moves the skin around the eyes can enact the cerebrum to examples of positive feelings. So grin and grin frequently! Even if you are having an awful day, grin anyway. It may very well help you with turning the day around. The effects on the cerebrum may release feel-good hormones that will cause you to feel better.

COLLAPSING YOUR ARMS

Crossing the arms is a resistance system to protect the heart and lungs. We regularly do it when we feel shaky, anxious, or disturbed. The physical obstruction gives others the signal that we are cut off and detached from them. Joining the arms across the body is an antagonistic body posture. A few investigations have indicated that crossing the arms can cause individuals previously industrious to feel like stopping their activities.

FORCE PRESENTING

One of the significant specialists in the zone of body language is Amy Cuddy. In her TedTalk, Cuddy talks about how body language can be the contrast between succeeding and coming up short at prospective employee interviews. She made members remain in high force stances and low force positions for two minutes before sending them into top-level talks with the condition. She estimated levels of the pressure hormone cortisol and the predominance hormone testosterone. The outcomes demonstrated that those remaining in high force positions had expanded higher degrees of testosterone and lower levels of cortisol than those in low force positions.

QUIT SLUMPING

This may appear glaringly evident; however, slumping not just influences your spine, it can also change your state of mind. Indeed, slumping can prompt back pain and irregular spine alignment. Intellectually, it can leave you feeling miserable, lacking vitality, and shut off from others. Sitting and standing up straighter can assist with settling back torment as well as lift your life and state of mind.

Changing your posture can be trying for your body from the outset, particularly on the off chance that you are accustomed to slumping over for significant periods such as when sitting at a desk all day. You may feel muscle aches in the neck, back, and behind – don't stress, this will pass! Meanwhile, I'd suggest utilizing Astrogel, a natural relief from discomfort cure containing new concentrates of arnica blossoms.

Improve your posture to improve your temperament

Body language likely isn't the first area you'd think to look at when you are experiencing a low state of mind. However, investigating our body language can reveal to us how we are truly feeling. Our body language has an immediate connection to our temperament. Similarly, our mindset influences our posture.

Simple ways you can fix your posture to adjust your state of mind:

1. Smile when you are having a terrible day.

2. Unfold your arms when you feel anxious and permit yourself to be available to circumstances.

3. Turning the palms of your hands forward when you walk will urge the shoulders to roll back as opposed to curling forwards towards a slump. This will improve your posture.

4. Power present before pressure instigating situations like prospective employee meet-ups.

Body language signs that someone is being deceitful

Untrustworthiness. It happens in many connections – and a great deal of the time, it accomplishes more mischief than anything. Once in a while, it is astute to keep insider facts from your partner in a relationship. You never need to keep your partner in the dark about a lot of things in your lives together. That is simply out and out insolent. It shows that you don't respect that person enough to recognize that they are deserving of the truth. You are saying that they aren't important enough to be told what's genuine – and that is, in every case, terrible in a relationship. You generally need to confess all to your companion, particularly about vital issues concerning your relationship.

However, many of us are childish. Sometimes, reality can be difficult to stomach. Now and then, a fact can place us in an uncomfortable condition of a burden once it's uncovered. So we will turn to a lie just to spare ourselves the discomfort of being yelled at or otherwise chastised. Your man may be blameworthy of doing this. He may be keeping you out of the loop about something that he ought to be opening up to you about.

This behavior is hazardous to a relationship. You can't hope to make your relationship work appropriately if you're not being taken care of in the best possible way. You need to ensure that you know all that is going on so you don't wind up getting tricked or bushwhacked by anything.

Men aren't generally the best verbal communicators. You may very well know this at this point. However, he will consistently tend to communicate through his body language and his physical actions whether he intends to or not. His intuition may disclose to you a lot of things about himself without him even meaning it. You simply need to ensure that you spot the signs when they present themselves. You need to keep an eye out in your relationship for these tell-tale ciphers. Here are some essential body language signs that indicate that your man is concealing something from you.

HE CROSSES HIS ARMS WHEN HE TALKS TO YOU.

He may not see that he's doing it. He's subliminally folding his arms since he's attempting to secure something. He wouldn't like to give all of you the way access. He's shutting himself off to you in a specific way. He wouldn't want to provide you with full access, and that is the reason he's utilizing his arms as a boundary.

HE DOES NOT FACE HIS BODY TOWARDS YOU WHEN YOU'RE CONVERSING.

It's conspicuous that he is attempting to conceal something if his body shifts towards another bearing when he's conversing with you. Rather than utilizing his arms as a method of safeguard, he just totally closes off access to you by dismissing you entirely.

HE DOES NOT LOOK STRAIGHT INTO YOUR EYES DURING CONVERSATIONS.

He doesn't need you to see the dread in his eyes. He doesn't want you to see the truth by looking straight into his spirit. The eyes are the windows to the soul after wall and he doesn't want you to see what is in his.

HE SEEMS EASILY IRRITABLE WHENEVER YOU ASK HIM QUESTIONS.

He gets hugely guarded when you ask him necessary questions about his life. He is going to cause it to appear as though you're investigating him when you're not. The weight is beginning to get to him, and he's going to wind up acting extremely irritable. He wouldn't like to get trapped in his falsehoods. Instead, he tries to divert the energy by being angry with you as though you've done something wrong.

HE ACTS ALL FIDGETY WHENEVER IT'S JUST THE TWO OF YOU.

He is eager. The mystery is genuinely squeezing him. There's such a significant amount of vitality within him that he needs to discharge it in one way or another. He needs to diminish the entirety of that pressure. That is the reason he will experience issues keeping still. He may make a misstep when it's just the two of you alone and there is no one else to help cover for him or distract away from his pressure.

HE TRIES TO MAINTAIN A VERY STRICT EXPRESSION ON HIS FACE ALL OF THE TIME.

He has a poker face on. Also, he's undoubtedly attempting to hide something – much like in poker. He doesn't need you to recognize what cards he's holding. He's keeping his cards hidden from everyone else, and he's under a great deal of pressure. Hence, the fidgeting, the anger, and now the poker face.

HE ACTS LIKE A BLINKING MACHINE.

Brain research has demonstrated that individuals who are lying or who are keeping secrets will, in general, blink at a quick rate. So be careful about the recurrence of his blinking. It could indicate that he is hiding something.

HE BITES HIS FINGERNAILS.

Brain research has additionally shown that the demonstration of gnawing fingernails is an indication of uncertainty or nervousness. On the off chance that he's restless about the secret he's hiding, he will be chewing his fingernails a great deal.

HE LASHES OUT AT YOU A LOT.

Everybody has a bad temper now and then but he's so blameworthy about the secret that he's hiding away and he realizes that it's inappropriate to keep something from you that he lashes out constantly. The blame is beginning to gobble him up inside. Also, he's attempting to carry on because of that blame. He will reverse the situation on you and cause it to appear as though you're the person who is hiding something. This puts him on edge and he will lash out at you for seemingly no reason.

UNDERSTANDING NON-VERBAL SIGNALS

Monitoring negative body language in others can permit you to get on implicit issues or awful emotions. Look for these negative non-verbal signs to detect what people are saying.

TROUBLESOME CONVERSATIONS AND DEFENSIVENESS

Troublesome or tense discussions are an awkward unavoidable truth we often face. Maybe you've needed to manage an annoying client, or expected to converse with somebody about their terrible showing. Or perhaps you've arranged a difficult agreement.

In a perfect world, these circumstances would be settled tranquilly. However, they are entangled by sentiments of apprehension, stress, or even resentment. Also, we may attempt to hide them. These feelings regularly appear in our body language. For instance, if somebody is showing at least one of the following signs, he will probably be withdrawn, uninvolved, or miserable:

- Arms collapsed before the body.
- Insignificant or tense outward appearance.
- The body some distance from you, more than is comfortable in normal conversation.
- Eyes down, keeping little or no contact.
- Avoiding engaging the audience.

At the point when you have to convey an introduction or to work together in a gathering, you need the individuals around you to be 100% cent locked in. Here are some "obvious" signs that individuals might be exhausted or distracted from what you're stating:

- Sitting drooped, with heads sad.
- Looking at something else or into space.
- Squirming, picking at garments, or tinkering with pens and telephones, composing or doodling.

Step by step instructions to Project Positive Body Language

At this point, when you utilize positive body language, it can add weight to the verbal messages or thoughts that you need to convey and help you to abstain from imparting blended or mixed signs. In this segment, we'll portray some fundamental postures that you can embrace to extend confidence and receptiveness.

ESTABLISHING A CONFIDENT FIRST CONNECTION

These tips can assist you in adjusting your body language, so you establish an extraordinary first impression.

Have an open posture.

Be loose. But never slouch. Sit or stand upright and place your hands by your sides. Resist resting your hands on your hips as this will cause you to seem more dominant which can convey animosity or a craving to rule.

Utilize a firm handshake.

However, don't become overly energetic! You don't need it to get unbalanced or, more regrettably, painful for the other individual. On the chance that it does, you'll likely seem to be impolite or forceful.

At the same time, you do not want to have a completely weak handshake. Somewhere nicely between is appropriate.

Keep in touch.

Try to maintain eye contact with the other person for a couple of moments straight. This will give her the impression that you're in tune and locked in. Be that as it may, abstain from turning it into a staring match!

Abstain from touching your face.

There's a typical discernment that individuals who touch their face or hair while addressing questions are being untrustworthy. While this isn't valid in every case, it's ideal to resist tinkering with your hair or contacting your mouth or nose, especially if your point is to seem to be reliable and trustworthy. The myth persists so just abstain.

PUBLIC SPEAKING

Positive body language can likewise assist you with engaging individuals, hiding introduction nerves, and exuding confidence when speaking in public. Here are several tips that can help you in doing this:

Have a positive posture.

Sit or stand upright, with your shoulders back and your arms straight and at your sides or before you. Try not to be tempted to place your hands in your pockets, or to slump or hunch as this will make you look undependable. You will look confident when you are standing with good posture and your head held upright.

Keep your head up.

Your head ought to be upstanding and level. Inclining excessively far forward or in reverse can make you look forceful or self-important, neither of which is becoming or desirable. Confidence with a slight touch of humbleness is given when your head is upright and level.

Practice and impeccable your posture.

You'd practice speaking your introduction in advance, so why not practice holding your body language, as well? Remain casual with your weight equally disseminated, knees slightly bent so you don't constrict the blood flow. Keep one foot somewhat before the other – this will assist you with maintaining your posture. Think first position in ballet if you're familiar with it. If not, become familiar with it.

Utilize open hand motions.

Spread your hands separated, before you, with your palms confronting marginally toward your crowd. This demonstrates an ability to convey and share thoughts. It also helps to turn your shoulders out which helps keep your back erect. Keep your upper arms near your body. Take care to maintain a strategic distance from overexpression, or individuals may give more consideration to your hands than to what you're stating.

Learn to Communicate Without Talking

While my formal degree is in mass communication, I have always considered myself a one-to-one communication graduate. Non-verbal contact fascinates me, perhaps better known as body language. Evidence follows multiple models and various theories as to what defines human communication, but they all conclude that body language communicates more than half of what we "think".

All our parents drilled into our heads the phrase, "actions speak louder than words", which is personified in the selling scenario. The communication between a salesperson and a customer involves giving and receiving wordless messages to and from both parties continuously. Next time you go to any shop, pay special attention to how (hopefully not "if") a salesperson welcomes you or knows you. Have they looked at you and made eye contact? Did you smile back? When you approached the counter, did they lean towards you or away from you? What did that little gesture "mean" about that salesperson, depending on which they did? Did you feel like you had faith in them? In setting the stage for continued (or discontinued) communication, these are normal, simple, and somewhat anticipated movements, but also very important. Take a moment today to watch employees from a distance in your shop. Which message would they send to the customer who just came in?

Strengthening relationships by helping you develop your non-verbal skills:

- Understand other people correctly, including the feelings they think and the unspoken signals they convey.

- Send non-verbal signals that suit your words to create trust and consistency in relationships.

- Respond to non-verbal signs showing others you understand, hear what they're saying, and care about their concerns.

Unfortunately, most people send misleading or derogatory non-verbal signals without even realizing it. When this occurs, our relationships lose both communication and trust. Trust has always been THE single most important element of a transaction. Lack of that item makes it much harder to close a sale.

I think most people would agree that our non-verbal abilities can be strengthened by everyone. To communicate better with the next person you talk to, one simple exercise is to pay particular attention to the color of their eyes as they speak. Doing so will allow you to study the face of that person and, more specifically, their eyes. This will, of course, allow you to concentrate even more intensely on what they say and convey a message that you are genuinely in tune with what they are trying to communicate.

You can see some very common possibilities in your showroom here. For example, we're going to use a boat store:

> Customer puts their foot on the boat or trailer - this shows a sign of staking out their claim saying "this is mine" (GOOD SIGN)

> Yawning-they're not focused on what you're saying (BAD SIGN)

> Feet pointing to the door - watch this after you pose a price - says they're going to get out (BAD SIGN)

It is important to note that for every single person, body language is not the same. No single action or characteristic tells the whole story. Still, the best way to make sure you pick up what they lay down is to ask questions.

CHAPTER 5: PERSONALITY TYPES

The Personality Types That Really Describe Behavior

The workplace is a place where we meet people who may be different from ourselves. It may be filled with people we wouldn't usually hang out with outside the workplace but we have no choice but to see them in the workplace every day. Therefore, understanding what the ten types of personalities you might meet at work are and how to deal with them is a good idea.

1. The Know It All

This person can't wait to correct you. To do so, they can even go out of their way. They may possess a lot of knowledge, but you hate how they always have to try to show you how intelligent they are.

Solution: The Know It All may be unaware of how annoying people find it when they contradict others. Tell them you understand that they're trying to help, but you'd rather find the answers on your own.

2. The Sniper

Through sarcasm, eye rolls, and rude remarks, the sniper excels. They're waiting patiently for a chance to jump in it to make you look poor.

Solution: Provide them with a taste of their own medicine and see how they react. Generally, it is their fear that makes them act in this way.

3. The Yes Person

This kind of person does not seem to have the courage to say no. They're doing things to please people all the time. It's entirely too easy to take advantage of this kind of person.

Solution: Typically, the Yes Person is a pleasant person. They can't say no because their boss and co-workers want to support them. Inform them that you know they're trying to be helpful, but that by handing too many things over and taking on too many, they end up delivering what no one wants.

4. The No Man

The No Man is the no person in direct contrast to the yes one. The No Man seems to be an expert in saping a group's energy and life. He spreads doom and gloom everywhere he goes at the sight of new ideas. No one likes the toxicity of him.

Solution: Explain that their negativity does not render any benefits to themselves or others. It only decreases the morale of all the others. Other colleagues can feel negative as well, but they get on with their work like everyone else. And so should he.

5. The Maybe Person

The Maybe Person may not seem to be able to make up his mind. He is an expert in procrastinating, hoping to avoid decision-making, delay plans, and cause frustration along the way.

Solution: Like the Yes Person, the Maybe Person may be pleasant. To avoid any conflict, they want others to make decisions for them. Explain that they are only delaying others from getting work done by avoiding making choices. In the end, everyone must make a choice, including the Maybe Person.

6. The Grenade

You must always try to stay on the good side of the grenade. When you are in their area, you don't want them to blow. What makes it worse is that, at the smallest things, they sometimes rant uncontrollably.

Solution: Grenades, deep down, just want to be respected. That's why they're asking for so much publicity. Explain (although gently) that they will never reach their ultimate goal of gratitude by shouting at people.

7. The Whiner

This individual loves having a good whine. They feel that life is unfair and there never seems to be anything going their way. They love spreading their suffering to others.

Solution: Empathize with how they feel and then guide them in a different direction. Tell them that instead of moaning with all that energy, it would be better to put it in another field that would help both themselves and others. Turn a negative into a positive.

8. The Tank

It's never a good idea to get the tank in the way. Their aggressive and angry behavior, as if you were flattened, could leave you psychologically wounded and paralyzed.

Solution: The Tank is a target of publicity like The Grenade and The Whiner. Let them know they won't be protected by their aggressive nature. They will never be accepted by this conduct, it only serves to push people away. Then try to stay out of their explosive way.

9. The Think They Know It All

This kind of person believes they've got all the answers. An optimistic, arrogant attitude makes people feel the Think They Know It All knows what they're talking about, but they're just as incompetent as anybody else.

Solution: Explain that, while sounding convincing and compelling, their exaggerations and half-truths are only wasting everyone's time. That's wrong. Tell them, politely, to mind their own business.

10. The Blank Wall

The Blank Wall (or no-one) seems to think nothing. They have a head in The Matrix that is reminiscent of Neo. With a blank stare and no verbal or non-verbal signals, this type of person appears to be self-restrained. Or simply not there.

Solution: The Blank Wall may want to hold himself aloof or may want to get involved, but he's too shy. We seem to be more open than most when faced with a blank wall. Next time you go for a drink or do something after work with your friends, invite the Blank Wall. Most probably they would enjoy it.

Understanding Personality types

- **Evitable Personality** — With strong social phobia, hypersensitive to criticism, and fear of people, this type of personality leads to loneliness. When put in low-level occupational positions, where little to no contact and personal interaction is needed, this type of employee can be very efficient and compliant. They are non-threatening and nondemanding, they usually have very few mates, if any. Often because they are too reluctant to react and hate confrontations, they are healthy and eager to take extra work. Such types of people are not antisocial, they are simply intimidated by people, particularly figures of authority. They don't have to be disciplined or micromanaged. Generally, they do all the work on time and make few mistakes. On the downside these "avoiding" workers will not work well in leadership positions and putting them in managerial roles can be a big mistake. They can be exploited and threatened easily and even submerged in illegal practices. These are best suited for jobs requiring minimal communication like clerical, administrative, computer engineering, web-based positions, accounting. They lack human connection and are therefore inspired by basic compassion, encouragement, and guidance. They are afraid they are misunderstood or rejected. They get along with everyone.

• **Dependent personality** - The narcissistic or borderline style director can do well. They need guidance and direction constantly. Their questions never cease and at every step of the way they need to be reassured. Because they have to be told constantly what to do, they make good assistants and can become good loyal employees when well educated. They're ready-made followers. They are worried that they will be hated or rejected if they make wrong choices and do not make good leaders. Frustrating and bureaucratic measures that can be used as a guide will need to be enforced on the downside. When left in charge, their indecisiveness and lack of direction will cost a fortune.

Approval is their psychological energy, so positive feedback can quickly inspire them. They can make trustworthy, loyal, and secure workers.

- **Histrionic temperament** – These types show a pattern of need for constant attention, anticipation. They have passion and enthusiasm. They're outstanding in management. They make great salespeople, speakers, performers, and teachers. Their lives are emotional roller-coasters. They rely on their instincts and go with their gut feelings. They love to be in front of crowds of people. They're the life of the party. They're kind and compassionate. Everyone is happier when they are happy but it can be a pleasure or a pain to work with them. They may change their mood suddenly. They may become furious, frustrated, and unhappy. They take it all personally and have an attitude that can be dangerous for all or nothing. They can cross the line in some cases and break the law.

They can make a fortune for your company but it's going to be a roller-coaster ride. Using their strengths, they can take the energy, excitement, imagination but provide as much information and direction as possible. They may need an assistant due to a lack of organizational skills. They must also be constantly reminded of the rules and policies of the organization. With their achievements, they are easily inspired but need a little guidance. When assessing their results, be patient and calm as they take it personally. You only need to say little to correct them. This type of person can quickly get angry and frustrated with overly dependent personalities asking too many questions but will fit well with employee avoidance and types of obsessive-compulsive personalities.

- **Borderline Personality** - "This is the best job I'll ever have and the worst place I've ever served." They're dangerously unstable, overly emotional, erratic, and impulsive. They make decisions that they later regret. You want to avoid hiring this person at all costs if you detect borderline personality because they can be vengeful. They expect you to believe what they believe and they'll get mad if you don't. They go from a high-manic state where they're full of energy, hope, and intense joy to rock bottom where they're depressed and suicidal. They can be nuts, neurotic, and they may need medical care. They feel they have the right to manipulate people and expect them to follow them. They love you or they hate you. There's no gray area - it's black or white. People are volatile and behave based on their current feelings. With stormy romances, drama, mood swings, impulsive spending, substance abuse, and poor health, their personal lives are typically messy. Many borderlines can be intelligent and professional and, if you are on their good side, can be a reliable employee. A sense of stability, consistency, and encouragement motivates them. They are dysfunctional, so in their personal and professional lives, they need someone to rely on. If you can build and give them a sense of security and purpose, you may be one of only a few people in their lives and they can give you all and be one of the best people you've ever had. During their performance evaluation, be calm and compassionate as it is easy to make them feel angry and resentful.

- **Narcissistic personality** – These people have feelings of entitlement, do not abide by the rules, think they are more intelligent or better than anybody else and have a sense of grandiosity. Generally, they feel they're more capable than others and feel they are hated. "It's my way or the highway! I'm unique and deserve to be popular. Others don't like me because they're jealous of my talents." They don't fit well within a corporate structure and sometimes make people excited with their agenda excited. They can be charismatic. They like to feel good at the detriment of others and think what is good for them is great for others. They tend to take things personally while they can be professional, clever, and impressive. If they feel betrayed, it is not unusual for them to indulge in vindictive behavior. They have a common propensity to control and exploit others for their personal good. Usually, they say more than they are, and they use coercion to undermine others. They also engage in illegal activities and can pose an enormous risk of liability. They see little use in self-improvement and continuing education around the world. Diplomatically, and often with ass-kissing, they need to be handled carefully.

Fragile self-esteem and deep feelings of guilt and inadequacy lie beneath the surface of the superficially bloated ego. When disciplined or fired, narcissists are likely to resort to malicious lawsuits and abuse. There must be cautious, tactful, respectful, and well-documented disciplining and firing for the protection of the employer.

- **The most dangerous form of antisocial personality in the working environment**. These types of people would do whatever it takes to reach their goals without any thought or remorse as to the detriment of everything and everyone. It's not always observable and can destroy the entire business. They're going to do absolute minimum work, take advantage of every profit, drive away customers. They will ruin prestige, exploit others in their unethical and illegal activities. Many of them become cutthroat businessmen with dubious schemes and greedy ways to go beyond everyone else. They can be aggressive, confrontational, disruptive, and impulsive. They would most likely be disqualified from being employed from the beginning by extensive criminal records.

- **Obsessive-Compulsive Personality** - This personality is committed to perfection and attention to detail. At the detriment of their social life, they usually thrive despite their work. They're scientists, planners, engineers, economists, reporters. With almost any type of personality, they will work well as they get the job done and that's their only concern. They are not confrontational or aggressive, and their plan is most often measured, coordinated, and centered. An obsessive-compulsive manager would be a good assistant with a dependable personality. They have high expectations on their own and make demanding managers. It's hoped that everyone will keep up the pace. They believe there is room for change at all times and take their job seriously. They also spend too much time "perfecting" the plan as workers, which can cause delays and need to be reminded of deadlines. They are inspired by the sense of accomplishment and give it 110%. Sometimes a sense of direction and deadlines need to be given to them as they can get lost in minute details and be indecisive about the course of the task. Working with them is the simplest and most rewarding type of people. The job is always done and there is no drama.

1. **Paranoid personality** – This type is characterized by an extreme lack of confidence and suspicion. They keep their guard up, and they don't open up easily. They assume that it is not possible to trust people. The world is full of cruel, greedy people who are going to hurt them and betray them. In general, in complex strategic planning, when they focus on work, they may achieve considerable success. They are also gifted with technical details, good memory, and strategic goals. Upon gaining confidence and security in their work environment, they will make good leaders. Expect intrusive questioning of the intentions of other

individuals and the reasons for their task. They like to hear calm rational explanations and do not respond well to guarantees or promises, but to reason. Always be honest in gaining confidence. Generally, they have sharp cognitive abilities and can immediately detect lies. A sense of entitlement and superiority powers delusional psychology, often in revenge for their subjective feeling of inferiority. They see industry as an area of challenge and have a defensive approach. They're ready to beat you in your own game: keep their friends close and their enemies closer. You never know what someone's agenda is. Managing suspicious workers may be difficult in extreme cases and it can create a stressful and aggressive working environment. If betrayed, you will be pursued and humiliated by the paranoid personality. Once on the hit list, a painfully plotted way out, your fate is sealed. They assume that nothing is their fault.

2. **Passive-Aggressive Personality** – This type believes life is not fair, nothing is their fault, something bad happens to them even if they do everything wrong, they are a victim, and that they always have "perfectly reasonable" explanations. They never take responsibility or behave like a party that has been hurt. Through their job, they are passive, practitioners of procrastination, and they use "self-handicapping" methods that they use as an excuse for not doing work. They are hostile, malicious, and can engage in sabotage, corporate espionage, malicious whistle-blowing,

and can sink into low company. They were eligible to sue for civil law. Be vigilant about firing this type of person, report and convey the reasons for your decision, and provide a face-saving way to leave the company. Eventually, this person will become the burden of someone else. To stop more lawsuits, be vigilant of guidelines.

The bottom line: Hire competent professionals who can get along well and get the job done to create an ideal work atmosphere. Carefully screen the candidates to remove any apparent troublesome people with substance abuse records, criminal history, litigation, poor record quality, or financial issues. They're just going to be trouble and a waste of time. Hire the right people — they're the ones that will make you good managers and employees and help the company grow.

CHAPTER 6: MANIPULATION

Psychological manipulation

Psychological manipulation is a sort of social influence that intends to change the conduct or impression of others through roundabout, misleading, or mischievous strategies. By propelling the interests of the controller, frequently to another's detriment, such techniques could be viewed as exploitative and shrewd. Social influence isn't necessarily harmful. For instance, individuals, companions, family, and specialists, attempt to convince to change unhelpful propensities and practices. Social influence is commonly seen to be innocuous when it regards the privilege of the influenced to acknowledge or dismiss it and isn't unduly coercive. Contingent upon the specific circumstance and motivations, social influence may, however, comprise mischievous manipulation.

Motivations of manipulators

Manipulators can have different potential motivations, including, yet not restricted to:

- The need to propel their motivations and individual addition at any expense to other people

- A substantial need to accomplish sentiments of intensity and prevalence involved with others

- A need to feel in charge

- A craving to increase a sentiment of control over others to raise their impression of confidence

- Weariness, or becoming sick of their environment, considering it to be a game more than harming others

- A secret plan, criminal, or something else, including monetary manipulation (frequently observed when the old or clueless, unprotected well off are purposefully focused for the sole motivation behind getting an unfortunate casualty's budgetary resources)

- Not identifying with hidden feelings, responsibility fear, and resulting legitimization (wrongdoer doesn't control intentionally, yet instead attempts to persuade themselves regarding the weakness of their feelings)

The weakness of psychopathic manipulators includes these thoughts as well:

- Subordinate individuals should be cherished and are guileless and at risk to express yes to something to which they should state no.

The victims are generally:

- Youthful - has debilitated judgment thus will, in general, accept misrepresented promoting claims.

- Credulous - can't accept there are unscrupulous individuals on the planet, or assumes that if there are any, they won't be permitted to go after others.

- Susceptible - excessively allured by charmers. For instance, they may decide in favor of the beguiling politician who kisses babies.

- Trusting - straightforward individuals frequently accept that every other person is straightforward. They are bound to concede to individuals they barely know without checking qualifications, and so forth., and more reluctant to address alleged specialists.

- Heedlessness - not giving an adequate measure of idea or consideration on mischief or blunders.

- Desolate - forlorn individuals may acknowledge any idea of human contact. A psychopathic stranger may offer human brotherhood at a cost.

- Narcissistic - narcissists are inclined to falling for ridiculous honeyed words.

- Imprudent - settle on the spot judgment calls about, for instance, what to purchase or whom to wed without counseling others.

- Charitable - something contrary to psychopathic: excessively legitimate, excessively reasonable, too compassionate.

- Thrifty - can't disapprove of a deal regardless of whether they know the reason it is so modest.

- Materialistic - simple prey for advanced sharks or pyramid schemes.

- Covetous - the hungry and exploitative may fall prey to a mental case who can without much of a stretch tempt them to act improperly.

- Masochistic - need a sense of pride, thus unwittingly let insane people exploit them.

- They think they merit it out of a feeling of blame or guilt or shame.

- The old - the older can wind up exhausted and less equipped for performing multiple tasks. When hearing an attempt to seal the deal, they are more reluctant to think that it could be a con. They are inclined to offering cash to somebody with a hard karma story.

Approaches to Stop Being Manipulated

Let's be honest: being controlled sucks.

Perhaps the main thing more terrible than being controlled is conceding skeletons in the closet. When we understand we've been had, we feel moronic, frail, and embarrassed. Furthermore, it doesn't end there. If we continue succumbing to their stunts, manipulators leave us with an awful feeling about our general surroundings. As opposed to being harmed once more, we may choose to confide in nobody. Or then again we may leave ourselves to the "reality" that a few people are takers and others are providers. In any case, one's lives are loaded up with dread and questions.

Try not to surrender – there is a superior way!

Manipulation possibly works when you neglect to remember it or permit it, at any rate. That is why this section contains things that you can do to perceive, stop, or avert being controlled. A portion of these thoughts may not be conceivable – or even alluring – in your circumstance. That is OK. Each individual and each circumstance is different. However, with these decisions, you're certain to discover a lot of ways that you can quit being controlled in your private or professional life.

So here they are, in no specific order:

1: Get to know yourself and your qualities.

If you don't have the foggiest idea of what is most important to you, you can't settle on choices that work for you. Also, notwithstanding when your choices are great ones, you'll question yourself. That uncertainty gives manipulators the preferred position they're searching for.

2: Take a couple of full breaths and ask yourself whose duty this is.

How frequently do your loved ones, even associates, request that you clean up their messes? Regard yourself – and them – enough to consider them responsible. Rescuing is for kids, little dogs, and individuals caught in uncontrollable circumstances. Not grown-ups. You're expected to save yourself. Superman is not going to do it for you.

3: Some individuals will say anything to get what they need. Quit trusting them. You know who they are... because they've deceived you previously. If you can't see through their falsehoods when you have to, stay away from them. Completely.

4: When somebody won't take no for an answer, tell yourself that it's your final answer – regardless of whether others acknowledge it or not. It generally feels better when individuals concur with you – or, if nothing else, acknowledge your entitlement to do what's best for you. However, nobody feels great all the time, and the cost of giving in is high. If your choice is important to you, stick with it. You needn't have anybody's permission to make the best choice for you.

5: Ask yourself what values are in question, and how significant they are. There's nothing wrong with trade-offs and exchanges – as long as your trustworthiness isn't on the table. It is better to say that you are managing a straightforward conscience issue, or is there something else to consider? If participating will leave you feeling objectified, powerless, or worse, consider your choice cautiously.

6: Take all the time you need to consider your choice. Making a rushed decision is a typical manipulation strategy. Furthermore, when the misery appears to be genuine, it's frequently because somebody other than you failed. If somebody needs something right this moment, tell them you're occupied. Refuse to be rushed. Their urgency is not your urgency. Take the time you need to make a careful decision. Don't allow yourself to be pressured.

7: Remember that not every person will like your choices, yet the individuals who matter will understand your right to make them. Individuals push you extremely hard for one of two reasons: either their qualities are in question, or they're just not concerned with yours. The individuals who genuinely care about you will treat your wants and needs with deference, understanding when it's complicated. The individuals who don't, do not merit stressing over.

8: Remind yourself of the significance of real love. Individuals who don't gain from their missteps are bound to repeat them. When we shield the individuals we care about from themselves, they quit developing. Furthermore, we continue expecting to protect them.

9: Instead of doing what's quickest or least demanding, consider the long-term results of your activities. Manipulators are incredible at making their choice the quickest, the most straightforward, or the least difficult. They're additionally very good at keeping us focused on how we're feeling at this moment. That is why we do things that we lament later. When you're enticed to do what feels better – or maintain a strategic distance from what feels awful – stop and think about what's to come. What will this mean to you (and those you care about) today around evening time, tomorrow, or one week from now? Envision yourself managing the outcomes, at that point, settle on a choice that considers all of this.

10: Make sure your trust is earned. Not every person is as well-meaning as you seem to be. You think about everybody's needs before settling on a significant choice. You approach individuals with deference. Furthermore, you would unquestionably never profess to be something you're most certainly not. However, a few people do that throughout the day. Feel free to trust in the integrity of human instinct – don't expect that nothing meddles with it. Watch new people for some time and focus on their collaborations. Not every person is as straightforward as you may be.

11: Refuse to draw in with menaces. A few people will attempt to scare you into making their offering. They may tear you down, change to a forceful tone, or attempt to panic you into accommodating them. Try not to give them an option to pull it off. When the discussion turns monstrous, leave. Let any individual who uses these strategies realize that the discussion is finished – and that it will remain so unless you're treated with respect.

12: Find out what's not being said. Manipulators only sometimes give you the entire story. If you're being approached to settle on an extreme choice, who benefits from it? What's the other side of the story? What's a feasible conclusion?

13: End dangerous connections. A dangerous relationship is sincerely harmful. If you commonly feel more awful about yourself in the wake of investing energy with your companion, what is that "fellowship" in light of? Investing energy with individuals who make a propensity for putting you down, making statements that lead you to question yourself, or suggesting that you should put them first isn't beneficial for you. Leave them if you can. If you can't, or don't have any initiative to, give some genuine thought to how much time you're willing to go through with them.

14: Don't let others make you responsible for their feelings. The way that somebody feels miserable, hurt, or furious about something you did doesn't imply that you weren't right. If somebody near you feels harmed by your words or activities, talk about it. Clear up any false impressions and apologize if you didn't think about somebody's feelings. At times, we need to do things that others won't like. Try not to alter your perspective or ask for forgiveness because somebody responds negatively.

15: Identify your most astounding qualities in every circumstance and ensure that you're considering them. If nothing is more essential to you than trustworthiness, don't lie for anybody. If the commitment is the thing that matters most to you, don't give anybody a chance to convince you to state or do whatever may hurt somebody you care about. Consider your most noteworthy qualities before settling on any significant choice, and you won't wind up doing things you regret later.

16: Take responsibility regarding your very own issues and demand that others do so as well. Is it normal to say that you are the individual everybody relies upon? Do others assume that you'll be there to rescue them? The arrangement is necessary (although not in every case simple). Stop taking responsibility for the missteps of others. If somebody you care about has failed, quit considering her to be an injured party who needs rescuing. Think about how conceivable it is that she's a competent grown-up who's searching for a simple way out. Let her realize that you can't take on her issues and that you have confidence in her ability to deal with her problems on her own. Offer to be a sounding board if she needs to investigate alternatives. Everybody needs to grow. Try not to turn into somebody's reason to stagnate.

17: Remember the price you pay for doing things that don't feel right to you. When you let others talk you into something against your "better judgment," you don't like yourself. What's more, you loathe them for thinking that you should put their wants and needs before yours. This damages both you and your relationship. Is it ultimately justified, despite all the trouble?

18: Stop running from your feelings. A few of us fear rejection. Others go down at the first trace of hostility. Still others can't deal with even a gentle regretful fit. Notice where you're the most powerless and face your fear. It takes boldness to manage exceptional feelings like dread, blame, and low self-esteem. However, it gets easier after some time. And the advantages endure forever.

19: If something doesn't feel right, it most likely isn't. Try not to give anybody the chance to work you out of your feelings. Your gut feeling is probably right. How often have you had that bothering feeling that something isn't right – and ignored it? What's more, how often have you thought twice about it? Trust your emotions to disclose to you that something's wrong. Then use your rationale to make sense of what it is.

20: Remind yourself that each 'yes' contains more than one 'no'. Clubbing with a friend means surrendering a peaceful night at home. Fulfilling one individual may mean frustrating another person. What's more, accomplishing something you're not happy with means disapproving of yourself. Before you consent to something, consider what you're sacrificing.

21: Remember that your life isn't intended to be a popularity contest with everybody getting a vote. We all have different qualities, different convictions, and different life experiences. If you let general opinions run your life, you're probably going to get up one morning, years from now, and wonder what happened to "your" life. Other people's endorsement is fine, but it won't give your life meaning. What's more, sometimes you'll truly miss it.

The most effective method to Stop Manipulation in the Workplace

Meeting a very overwhelming person in the working environment is normal. It could be your boss, another person's supervisor, your coworker, or even somebody lower in the chain of importance of your association. This manipulative person can overwhelm us, make us feel stifled, and make us weak. We can even lose our feeling of self-worth and feeling of importance, and inevitably we will feel powerless and debilitated. The best way to stay away from manipulation is to take our power back and engage ourselves.

The following are simply the guidelines while in transit to empower ourselves and, at last, quit being manipulated in the workplace.

- Recognize that you are being manipulated. If you don't understand and acknowledge that you are being manipulated and being pushed around by somebody, you will think that it's difficult to change and do the subsequent stages to stop it. You should know about what's going on with you and your environment.

- Assume responsibility for your life. You can't control anybody. The only person you can control is you. Recognize how you feel under the circumstances and start settling on choices and organize the significant things to you.

- Set objectives. Envision how you might want things to be. Defining objectives will assist you in focusing on what is critical to you. These objectives might be huge or tiny. Regardless of the size, they are still objectives, and this is imperative to decision making, so you have a marker of where you are, what your goals are, and how to get there. Try not to give anybody a chance to hurt your odds of meeting them.

- Express your thoughts, considerations, and inclinations. Once you set your objectives, you need to express them so anyone can hear you and the next person or individuals, so they realize where you stand. Be clear when you express your objectives. Try not to expect immediately that the other person comprehends what you are stating. You must be prepared to clarify different issues.

- Hold fast. Hesitation won't help. Try not to avoid what you accept, feel, or need. Be firm on your choices and finish your arrangements and objectives.

- Quit sitting tight for other people's endorsement. If we generally look for the endorsement of other individuals, we will be manipulated continuously. If you regard yourself and go to bat for what you need, others will begin regarding you as more significant for it.

- Give up. A portion of your goals may not occur and may not be relevant. You may understand that there indeed exists an uneven relationship. Honestly, we can't change others, but we can change ourselves. If the person doesn't respect your choices, at that point, think about that person as a poisonous person that you need to maintain a strategic distance from. Acknowledge and conclude that you cannot allow them to trouble you. Discover ways to guarantee that you deal with yourself only. Acknowledge them for what their identity is, and start engaging yourself to be the person that you need to be.

- Try not to look out for others to enable you. You only need your own permission and nobody else's.

- We are altogether defenseless against being manipulated in relationships, regardless of whether between romantic partners, companions, guardians, children, bosses, collaborators, or neighbors. When we enable someone else to manipulate us, we are plotting with their craving to control our emotions, intentions, and even our considerations through tricky, exploitative, and out-of-line implications. A manipulative relationship is uneven and unequal, propelling the objectives of the controller to the detriment of the person being manipulated. These relationships become disruptive after some time. If you need to change this sort of relationship, you should initially perceive the highlights of manipulation and, after that, search inside to comprehend your commitment to the manipulation. There are compelling approaches to face manipulation and bring equalization once more into the relationship.

- Manipulation isn't equivalent to power. We, as a whole, use power with other individuals to propel our objectives, and this is one of the signs of sound social working. Power perceives the rights and limits of other individuals, and it depends on immediate, legitimate correspondence. The effect is one way we have of working adequately on the planet. Power perceives the trustworthiness of the other person, including the privilege not to oblige the endeavored influence. Manipulation, however, relies upon hidden motivation and an endeavor to force someone else into yielding. Although it might create the impression that the controller is solid and in charge, there usually is instability under the façade. The inclination to misuse others and negligence of their privileges is an indication of unfortunate personality working. Indeed, individuals who manipulate others experience issues in keeping up great interpersonal relationships.

- The individuals who manipulate other individuals are great at spotting individuals to control. If they feel unfit to manipulate somebody, they, for the most part, surrender and proceed onward to another person who is bound to be responsive to the endeavored manipulation. When you perceive the highlights of the manipulation, the subsequent stage in amending the circumstance is to find your very own commitment to the issue. (This announcement may appear to be somewhat difficult to acknowledge. The controller has the issue, you may state. Understand that manipulation can't happen in a vacuum. As is valid for any relationship, it takes two parties.) You can come to comprehend your commitment to the manipulative circumstance and afterward find a way to address it.

Here are some traits of the individuals who are defenseless against manipulators:

- You feel helpful and adored when you can deal with the necessities of other individuals. This goes past being pleasant to other individuals. Your feeling of worth is tied up in getting things done for other people. You take this so long that you please other individuals to the detriment of your own prosperity. For instance, you may purchase something particularly pleasant for your partner or a companion when you could never spend that sort of cash on yourself. Manipulators are attracted to this sort of person and have no doubts about exploiting this specific personality characteristic. You need the endorsement and acknowledgment of other individuals. Albeit, the vast majority value being acknowledged, an issue happens when you feel that you should be acknowledged by everybody consistently. The center issue here is the dread of being rejected or relinquished – and it is solid to such an extent that you would successfully maintain a strategic distance from the sentiments related to this dread. The controller works by giving you the acknowledgment that you need – and after that, taking steps to pull it back.

- You dread communicating negative feelings. Although communicating outrage and participating in contention are rarely charming, a few people will go to any length to maintain a strategic distance from an encounter. They need things to be pleasant consistently. They fear that they will self-destruct amid negative feelings. Manipulators have a simple errand in this sort of relationship – they should take steps to raise their voice, and afterward, they get their way.

- You can't state no. One of the qualities of a solid relationship is proper limits that clarify what your identity is and a big motivator for you. To keep up solid limits, in any case, you should in some instances state no when somebody endeavors to push your cutoff points. If you fear the contention that may emerge when you say no, you play under the control of the controller. Learning successful emphatics techniques is an approach to recapture your feeling of control in a manipulative relationship.

- You come up short on your very own firm feeling self. A reasonable feeling of self implies that you realize what your qualities are, what your identity is, a big motivator for you, and where you start, and the other person begins. If you have an unsure feeling of self, it is difficult to be confident in your own judgment or to settle on choices that work to support you. Without a reasonable understanding of yourself, you might be an obvious choice for a controlling manipulator.

- When you are in a manipulative relationship, it is useful to perceive the personal propensities that enable the other person to declare control over you. You can come to understand and investigate these securely with the help of an expertly prepared advisor. While you will most likely be unable to change the conduct of the controller, you can change your very own reactions to submit to manipulation with the goal that you accomplish your very own firmer feelings respectably. The misery coming about because of a manipulative relationship can prompt life-changing encounters that create knowledge and the capacity to adapt all the more successfully to the requests of ordinary living.

Step by step instructions to manipulate anyone

Manipulating others is an approach to get what you need, regardless of whether it is tricking your manager into giving you a raise or getting your lover to whisk you away on a nostalgic outing. Many acknowledge this to be inappropriate and wrong. The fact is, it is a part of everyday life and everyone participates in manipulative behavior at some point.

Whatever your purpose behind manipulating someone, play your cards right, and hone your manipulation skills. Assess an assortment of manipulation techniques and make sense of how to manipulate individuals in any situation. If you have to make sense of how to manipulate others quickly, then you can cry a fake tear and seek after these methods.

- Take an acting class. A significant bit of manipulation is making sense of how to play your emotions and cause other individuals to react to your made estimations. If you have to acknowledge how to appear more disturbed than you are or to use an assortment of other energetic techniques to get your way, then taking an acting class is a perfect method to improve your powers of impact. Do whatever it takes not to tell other individuals that you're taking an acting class if you're doing it to make sense of how to manipulate individuals. Else they may become suspicious of your strategies instead of confiding in you.
- Take an exchange or open talking class. While acting classes can empower you to express your emotions and induce others to allow you to have what you need, taking a dialog or open talking class will enable you to make sense of how to persuade other individuals. Not only will you make sense of how to form and express your thoughts in a more helpful manner, but you'll also learn techniques for making your needs singularly convincing.

- Set up likenesses. You can do this by a system called 'pacing,' where you can mirror the other person's non-verbal communication, your sound model, and so on. This tranquil and compelling procedure is phenomenal for inducing your chief or colleagues to achieve something. Being eager may not work in a specialist setting.

- Be charismatic. Charismatic individuals have a trademark tendency to get what they need. If you have to manipulate individuals, need to work your attraction. You should have the ability to smile and light up a room, have congenial non-verbal communication to make individuals want to banter with you. You should also have the ability to talk with absolutely anyone, from your nine-year-old cousin to your history teacher.

  o Here are some different approaches to being charismatic:

    1) Make individuals feel special. Look at them when you speak with them and get some information about their feelings and interests. Demonstrate to them that you care about getting close to them — regardless of whether or not you actually do.

    2) Emanate assurance. Charismatic individuals love what their personality is and what they do. Besides, if you believe in yourself, individuals will be inclined to focus on you and to respect your needs.

3) Make certain when you state something, regardless of whether it's real or just a single additional creation, do it with conviction. Endeavor to be talkative while staying strong with your subject.

- Gain from the managers. If you have a companion, relative, or even an enemy who is an expert manipulator, you ought to observe this individual and take notes. See how they get what they need. This will give you new insight into how to manipulate individuals. If you're genuinely committed to making sense of how to manipulate other individuals, you may learn something from this person.

- Figure out how to watch others. Every individual has different excited and mental stimulations and is, hence, manipulated for different reasons. Before plotting your latest manipulation scheme, put aside the reasons to think about the individual you want to manipulate. Grasp what is most critical to him and see the best approach for getting this person to bend to your needs.

  a   Here are some different things you may find when you read individuals:

  1) Some individuals are helpless against emotional responses. These individuals

are emotional themselves, cry at movies, love doggies, and have considerable powers of compassion and empathy. To get them to do what you need, you'll have to play to their emotions until they feel disappointed about you and give you what you need.

2) Other individuals have a strong guilt reflex. Some people were raised in a prohibitive family where they were rebuked for doing each not entirely obvious detail wrong and now experience life feeling guilty about pretty much everything that they do. With these individuals, the appropriate response is undeniable — make them feel frustrated about not giving you what you need until they yield.

3) And some individuals are dynamically open to the goal system. If your companion is all around legitimately objected, scrutinizes the news habitually, and, in every case, find facts and verification before choosing a decision, then, you'll have to use your

calm alluring powers to get what you need rather than utilizing your feelings to manipulate him.

How to manipulate girlfriend

Manipulating a romantic partner is a whole different game. I warn you, some of these are ugly. Use what you can with a good conscience. If you're a real 'player', you won't care. You'll use them all and then just throw away a good woman. No wonder so many women think men are dogs.

Use Eye Contact to Manipulate Women into Liking You

When you are attempting to manipulate women with low confidence into enjoying you, the main point will be to hold extended eye contact with her. If you are attempting to fool her into loving you, eye contact can do wonders. Make it look natural and let her know that you are into her. Try not to make a clumsy attempt and wind up looking unpleasant. Make sure it sends her the correct message.

Demonstrate a Little Interest In Her

Women get all the attention they need. Men may appear to be frantic, especially when they are with pretty women.

Along these lines, if you will, in general, demonstrate no enthusiasm for her, it will drive her nuts. While at the bar, make sure she sees you however, notice and then disregard her presence. This may make her inquisitive and might make her marvel 'why isn't he intrigued by me?' This is one of the manners in which you can manipulate women with low confidence.

Get *Her* To Notice *You*

When attempting to manipulate low confidence women into enjoying you, make her come to you. Never allow women to look over you and reject you. It is time you bring things into your hands. Attempt to get her to see you by contradicting her. Let her realize her decisions weren't right or she has committed an error. Along these lines, she won't just see you but will attempt to intrigue you and demonstrate to you that she was correct in wanting your attention.

Envy Can Manipulate Women With Low Self-Esteem

Having met the young lady you had always wanted, and if you are attempting to fool her into being your better half, you have to make her envious. Envy can make any young lady hopelessly enamored. The dread of losing somebody will make you hold her complete attention. Along these lines, whenever your objection of affection is near, be coy with different young ladies to make her desirous. This is one of the manners in which you can manipulate women with low confidence into wanting you.

Attempt To Confuse Her

If you need to get the young lady, you like to be your better self, consistently send her mixed signals. Never be clear with your method for communicating your feelings for her. Make her feel loved while simultaneously make it look easygoing. She should feel mistaken for what is happening with you. She should attempt to make sense of the feelings you have for her. Who wouldn't like to feel loved? So does your young lady. She will need to know whether she is being loved or it is was your pleasant nature. This is one of the approaches to manipulate your woman with low confidence into preferring you.

Be A Little Mysterious

To get women to be inquisitive, you have to look somewhat secretive. Be a little shrouded - never let her know too much about you. Give a couple of insights yet never uncover anything completely. Utilize her interest to grow more enthusiasm for you. By being secretive, you compel her to think about you, which builds up excitement for you. In this way, consistently appear to be a little mysterious when she is near. This is one of the manners in which you can easily manipulate your woman into wanting you more.

Make Her Feel Left Out To Manipulate Her

When attempting to manipulate your young lady into loving you, you have to make her feel left out. Be decent to everyone around her, however, don't try to chat with her. Along these lines, you will make her feel left out. This will make her feel that there is an issue with her that you dislike so she may attempt to stand out enough to be noticed notwithstanding when this sort of makes her disappointed with you. When you give her your attention, she may receive it with a great deal of delight.

Be Commanding When You Try To Manipulate Women

When attempting to manipulate women with low confidence, be overwhelming. Set your predominance and take control to let her know where she stands when you date her. Tell your intended that you have a single happy life and that you cherish it so she can understand what to do and what not to do. The way you set the boundaries, the more joyful you can be. Never consistently allow her to control, rather take things in your grasp and set limits.

Get Her Sympathy Vote

When you need to manipulate your low confidence woman into enjoying you, then you have to get her compassion. Women show sympathy, and when utilized at the ideal time, you stand out enough to be noticed and caring. Disclose to her a sad story that has transpired. Put in a little dramatization and attempt to get her sympathy. Let her realize that you have a few sorrows and how you have defeated those battles. By doing this, you get the opportunity to have a soft spot in her heart.

Concede That You Are In Love With Her

Everybody wants to be informed that they are loved. Along these lines, tell your woman that you are infatuated with her. Uncover the little secret to your sweetheart, however, don't anticipate that she should give you any returns immediately. Disclose to her that she is loved so deeply and that she has consistently been the one for you. Women have confidence in head over heels love, and they welcome it when there is a great deal of show in it. This is one of the manners in which you can manipulate your woman who has low confidence into enjoying you.

Be Confident When Trying To Manipulate Women

Women love confident men, and it is a central point that draws them in. To make yourself adored, you should be a confident person who merits being around. Carry on with your life such that she feels she should be with you. Make her feel that being with you may make her life significantly more interesting. If you need to manipulate your low confidence woman into enjoying you, then you should be a confident person.

Play HardBall

When you need to manipulate your young lady into loving you, you have to play the hardball game. Make her feel that you are bothersome and never extremely simple to intrigue or you are way out of her group. Turn her down when she requests a drive home, to fix her vehicle or when she invites you for espresso. By dismissing her favors or demands, you make her feel that you are somebody special and that she should make a decent attempt to get you. This is one of the approaches to deceive your woman with low confidence and make her strive harder to get you.

Make Her Feel That You Are Amazing

If you need to make the young lady you had always wanted as your lover accept that you are astonishing, demonstrate to her how amazing her life will be when she is with you. Make her feel that her life with you is far superior to her dream. If you make her accept that life with you can be bold and exciting, a woman with low confidence will, in general, begin to look all starry-eyed at you. This is one of the approaches to manipulating your woman with low confidence.

Make Physical Contact With Her

When you have a sentimental enthusiasm for your low confidence woman to manipulate her into enjoying you, you have to take your time. She will never understand your advances unless you make physical contact with her. Touch her, stroke her, make it look normal and easygoing. Give the subtle clues that you have feelings for her. Women with low confidence can be easily manipulated into preferring you with this straightforward trick.

Work On Her Emotions To Manipulate Her

To manipulate a woman with low confidence, you have to comprehend her feelings better. You have to watch how she responds to different circumstances. Use a little skill to manage her, recognize what will make her happy, or what will make her miserable. Toss in happy memories of hers and make her happy and, in a split second, review a tragic memory and make her miserable. Along these lines, you can easily figure out how to control her by controlling her emotions, utilizing her feelings.

Be A Little Dramatic

Women will in general fall for the man who makes stupendous motions to demonstrate their adoration. Along these lines, if you need to manipulate her into loving you,

you have to demonstrate to her that you adore her with a great deal of dramatization. Overwhelm her; make it a major ordeal when it comes to communicating your advantage. It will help you in winning her heart easily, and she will give you a chance to take complete control of her life. This is one of the manners in which you can manipulate your woman who has low self-confidence.

Make Her Listen to You

To cause your lady to hear you out, all you need is to express your feelings; glad ones, irate ones, or even dismal ones. Let her comfort you. The more troubled you feel, the more sympathy you will get from her. The more joyful you express your very own self; the more pleasure you get from her. When in fierceness, she should reflect your temperament, and ideally, you will wind up having a decent time with her. Never be the person who consistently tunes in to her stories, cause her to tune in to yours most of the time. This is one of the approaches to manipulate women with low confidence into preferring you.

Make A Move Unexpectedly

When out on the town with your lady, when the pressure gets the opportunity to build, draw in her. Make a startling move, snatch her in the arms and kiss her for a second or two and leave her needing more. Keep in mind, you get just one chance either to intrigue her or make her run, so make it a good one. This is one of the most effortless and amazing ways you can manipulate women with low confidence into loving you.

Be Online But Never Respond Immediately

To make women insane, you have to send an instant message or even visit over internet social media like Facebook or Hangouts and never react right away. Leave her expecting messages from you. You have to have an extraordinary discussion with her and afterward use this method. If you leave her with no answer following having begun the discussion, it probably won't be compelling. In this way, begin a fascinating discussion and after that don't react to her right away. Be online, yet give her a deferred reaction. It will drive her nuts. This is one of the most well-known patterns to manipulate women with low confidence.

Try not to See Her Regularly

If you need your woman to yearn for you, you ought to never be too accessible to her. Make it a point never to meet her or see her all the time. Avoid a day or two in the middle so she builds up interest to see you again and she will be compelled to consider why you have not shown up. This is another approach to manipulate women with low confidence.

Reveal to Her She Is Different

Women love to feel unique and special yet men neglect to make them feel this way. To manipulate a low confidence woman, reveal to her that she is different from every one of the women you have met up until this point. Reveal to her that she is the woman you have consistently longed for. Be sure she understands that you accept that she is somebody unique from all the other women you have met up until now. By doing this, you can, without much of a stretch, manipulate your woman into loving you.

Support Her

When attempting to manipulate women with low confidence, go to bat for her. Whenever she is censured or being made to feel poorly by others, back her up. Never give others a chance to tear her down. Along these lines, you will effortlessly dazzle your lady with low confidence as she may have her very own weaknesses. By going to bat for her, you promise her that you can guard her in space. And you will look like her very own knight in shining armor.

Mirror Her Actions

If you need your low confidence lady to enjoy you, reflect her activities. By doing this, you intrigue her and you can lure her into preferring you. By pacing her, you send her a subtle message that you are into her. Mirror her non-verbal communication, her feelings. This will assist you with making her vibe uncommon and she will begin to like you. Along these lines, if you are pondering approaches to manipulate low confidence women into enjoying you, this is probably the simplest way.

Vanish For A Few Days

In the wake of becoming acquainted with your young lady, if you need her to miss you terribly, then you have to vanish from her for a couple of days. Make it a point not to send her a message or call her when you have vanished. Advise your companions not to give away any information about you. She will attempt to contact you and start searching for you and will miss you when you are nowhere to be found. This is one of the approaches to manipulate your lady into enjoying you.

Be Charming

Everybody loves to be with individuals who are beguiling, carefree, and a determined worker. Be that sort of individual when you are around your low confidence lady. Continuously be sweet and have a gigantic grin all over to manipulate her into thinking you are cute. Love yourself. Any woman will go gaga for you if you truly love yourself.

This is one of the approaches to manipulate women into loving you.

Think Before You Act

Since you understand now the ways to manipulate low confidence women into preferring you, it isn't necessarily fitting to do this. She probably won't be in love with the person you really are but with the person you've pretended to be. Thus, the issue with manipulating a lady into loving you is that she may like you yet this will never keep going for a long-haul relationship. Along these lines, ensure that you have considered both the upsides and downsides before you really execute the ways for manipulating your lady into loving you. If you feel that the relationship is justified, despite all the trouble, it is smarter to work your sentiments out and go out on the town. If you feel the relationship isn't justified, despite any potential benefits then you can try it out.

Manipulating people is an ugly business. People can really get hurt. Be careful before you act. Be sure you know what you're doing and why.

Ways Manipulators Use Emotional Intelligence for Evil

Emotional intelligence is the same old thing. Indeed, the term was authored during the 1960s, and advanced by psychologists in later decades. The idea of emotional intelligence — which is characterized as an individual's capacity to perceive feelings and utilize that data to direct necessary leadership - has been around as long as we have.

This aptitude we allude to as emotional intelligence (otherwise called EI or EQ) resembles some other capacity: you can develop it, work to improve it, hone it. What's more, it's essential to realize that, much the same as different aptitudes, emotional intelligence can be utilized both morally and dishonestly.

The clouded side of emotional intelligence

Different ways emotional intelligence can be utilized against you. These activities and attributes don't generally identify an absence of morals; an individual may rehearse them accidentally. In any case, expanding attention to these practices will prepare you to manage them deliberately, and hone your own EQ as well.

1. They play on dread.

A manipulator will overstate actualities and overemphasize specific details in an attempt to alarm you without hesitation.

Methodology: Beware of claims that suggest you need mental fortitude or endeavors and impart a dread of passing up a great opportunity. Ensure you have all the details of a circumstance before making a move.

2. They misdirect.

We all value straightforwardness and trustworthiness, yet manipulators conceal reality or attempt to demonstrate to you just one side of the story. For instance, consider the chief or worker who intentionally spreads unverified bits of gossip and tattle to increase a vital bit of leeway.

Procedure: Don't believe all that you hear. Or maybe, base your choices on legitimate sources and pose inquiries when details aren't clear.

3. They exploit you when you're cheerful.

Frequently, we're enticed to say yes to anything when we're in a particularly positive mindset or jump on circumstances that look great at the time (however, we haven't had time to consider). Manipulators realize how to exploit those states of mind.

Technique: Work to expand the consciousness of your positive feelings the same amount as your negative feelings. When it comes to deciding, endeavor to have balance.

4. They exploit correspondence.

Manipulators know it's harder to say no if they accomplish something for you - - so they may endeavor to complement or flatter you, or say yes to little favors...and then approach you for enormous ones.

System: For sure, giving brings more happiness than getting. But on the other hand, it's imperative to know your limits. Also, don't be reluctant to say no when appropriate.

5. They push for home-court advantage.

A manipulative person may demand you meeting an associate in a physical space where the person can practice more strength and control. These individuals may push to consult in a space where they feel proprietorship and comfort, similar to their office, home, or some other spot you may feel less comfortable.

Methodology: If you have to make arrangements, offer to do so in a neutral space. If you should meet the individual on their home turf, request a beverage of water and take part in the casual discussion upon entry, to enable you to get your orientation.

6. They pose loads of questions.

It's anything but difficult to discuss ourselves. Manipulators know this, and they exploit it by posing test questions with a veiled motivation - finding concealed shortcomings or information they can use to further their potential benefit.

System: obviously, you shouldn't accept wrong thought processes in everybody who needs to become better acquainted with you. However, be careful with the individuals who pose questions while declining to share similar information about themselves.

7. They talk rapidly.

On occasion, manipulators will talk at a quicker pace or utilize uncommon jargon and language trying to pick up a bit of leeway.

Technique: Don't be hesitant to request that individuals rehash their point, or rephrase for clearness. You can likewise rephrase their point in your own words or request that they name a model - enabling you to recapture control of the discussion.

8. They show negative feelings.

A few people deliberately raise their voice or utilize solid non-verbal communication to show they're disturbed with an end goal of controlling others' feelings. (Ball coaches are experts at this.)

System: Practice delay. If somebody exhibits forceful feelings, pause for a minute before responding. In certain cases, you may even leave for a couple of minutes, allowing them time to cool off and get their emotions under control. Their feelings of escalation are probably not real so you are simply showing them that you are not buying into their drama.

9. They give you an amazingly restricted time to act.

An individual may attempt to compel you to settle on a choice inside a truly absurd amount of time. In doing so, the person needs to force you into a choice before you have an opportunity to gauge the results. Or even think through a decision. This is a high-pressure sales technique. Don't fall for it.

Technique: Don't submit to absurd requests. If your accomplice does not give you additional time, you're in an ideal situation to search for what you need elsewhere. Let them know that that is exactly what you intend to do.

10. They give you the silent treatment.

"By intentionally not reacting to your calls, instant messages, text messages, or different requests, the manipulator presumes control by making you pause, and plans to place uncertainty and vulnerability in your psyche," says Ni. "The silent treatment is a head game, where silence is utilized as a type of the influence."

Methodology: After you've endeavored correspondence to a sensible degree, give your accomplice a due date. In circumstances where choices are inaccessible, a straight-to-the-point discourse tending to their correspondence style might be relevant.

Placing it into training:

There will consistently be individuals who work to build their emotional mindfulness - in both themselves as well as other people. At times, they'll utilize that power for manipulative impact. Furthermore, that is why it is necessary for you to hone your emotional intelligence- - to secure yourself from their manipulations when they do.

Habits of Manipulative People

It very well may be difficult to distinguish whether somebody is manipulative upon first meeting them. Sadly, their childish nature regularly goes unnoticed until you've turned out to be too excessively engaged with their lives to leave suddenly. When they've drawn near to you, these Machiavellian rogues will do anything it takes to keep you around, for the sole purpose of utilizing you somehow. Maybe the most noticeably awful piece of being stuck in a manipulative friendship is that it makes you question the validity of others, which can mean continually re-thinking any other connections.

If you have a "companion" who shows these manipulative qualities, you should attempt to remove them from your life as quickly as possible.

They play guiltless

Manipulators have a method for playing around with reality to depict themselves as the innocent party.

They justify their conduct.

In addition to not taking their companions' recommendations, manipulative individuals cause their negative conduct to appear the main choice. They cause it to appear to you that they settled on the correct choice, although you know better from a target perspective. They regularly try to "win" arguments, as opposed to going along with the other party. The suggestion here is that they weren't tuning in to what you needed to state by any stretch of the imagination. They were hanging tight for you to finish your statement so they could offer an answer, paying little mind to how solid your recommendation was.

They change the subject frequently.

Since manipulative individuals genuinely care about themselves *only*, they, at last, will control discussion toward their very own needs any opportunity they get. They'll do this particularly when they realize they're off-base about something yet would prefer not to let it be known. Along these lines, rather than approving the other individual's sentiment, they'll change the subject to something harmless or generally random to the past theme. This causes them to maintain a strategic distance from reality in an indirect manner that is genuinely unnoticeable to other people.

They tell misleading statements.

Manipulative individuals will in general form reality to further their potential benefit. They'll regularly shroud information that they realize will uncover them as liars, going about as though this is by one way or another superior to telling a straight-out untruth. Manipulators approach all cooperations as though they're in an official courtroom, where what they state can be utilized against them.

They actuate blame

Alongside asserting honesty, manipulative individuals likewise make others feel remorseful. There might be times seeing someone where you don't have the opportunity or energy to manage certain circumstances, and the manipulative individual will make you have a feeling that you're "not there for him." They may even get you to set your well-being aside for later so they'll have someone to grumble to and look for guidance from (exhortation which they may not regard, at any rate).

They insult others

Manipulators are discourteous and grating naturally. Every genuine companion can feel good disturbing each other by jabbing fun harmlessly, however, manipulative individuals go over the edge with the pokes and affronts. They do this in social circumstances to noticeably undermine others and build up a feeling of strength. Manipulators never got over that secondary school mindset where it was "cool" to ridicule others and make them feel little by utilizing only their words.

They menace others

Manipulative individuals are menaces. This goes past abuse and frequently includes estrangement and the spreading of bits of gossip. Once more, this is whimsical conduct. However, it is regularly displayed by youthful, manipulative grown-ups. Activities, for example, disregarding certain individuals in a gathering, not giving them a chance to voice their assessments, or deserting them are a portion of the more "grown-up" approaches to menace. Manipulators will utilize these strategies to set up dominance. In truth, these individuals are amazingly hesitant and have low confidence, and will hurt anybody around them to rest easy thinking about themselves.

They limit their conduct

Manipulators cause it to appear as though their words and deeds are "not unreasonably huge an arrangement." Ironically, more often than not it's them who have overemphasized things. That is until they hear something they don't care for and reverse the situation on the other party. They don't demonstrate any sympathy for the individuals who have invested significant time and vitality attempting to support them and instead shift the fault onto every other person. They realize they have an issue. However, they cause it to appear as though the world's out to get them and not the other way.

They accuse others

Manipulators shift fault always. They skate through life without taking any responsibility regarding their activities. They either level out, don't concede they did anything wrong, or have some clarification to make their activities sound sensible given the conditions. Manipulative individuals don't live by any code of morals, and when it makes up for lost time with them, they'll point the finger anyplace else aside from at themselves.

Now you know the characteristics of manipulative people. Hopefully, you can avoid being their victim.

CONCLUSION

Personality analysis from body language is an art. And having positive body language is a blessing. Hence, it's profoundly essential to have appropriate body expression and posture while talking in front of an audience before a crowd of people and even individuals. Body language is significant in all types of communication. It assists with breaking the obstruction of newness and assists with shaping superior communication.

Understanding body language can go far toward helping you communicate better with others and decipher what others may be attempting to say to you. While it might be enticing to dissect signals individually, it's critical to take a look at these non-verbal signals comparable to verbal correspondence, other non-verbal signs, and the circumstances.

Feeling comfortable in any social interaction is an important element in attracting the opposite sex. Girls will easily pick up on it, and it's the best way to get them attracted to you. Through a lengthy series of positive experiences and results, trust is something you build up over the years. Thankfully for you, there are some things you can do to give the impression that you're instinctively confident and relaxed around women, even though you haven't built it up since childhood. There's also the complex "fake it until you make it." The more of these characteristics you display, the more they become part of you, and you will begin to feel more comfortable. At first, it will make you feel uncomfortable, as these are habits you are not used to. But soon, they will become a part of you. Yet remember: you don't want to be rude or cocky.

1. Presume Attraction: You should presume that she is already attracted to you when you first talk to a woman. Trust it. Believe it. It will make it much more congruent with everything you do and say. Confident guys think every woman is drawn to them already.

2. Body Language: If you speak to her, use deliberate gestures. Don't flail your neck about. Don't be mad, even though you're nervous. Good body language becoming an unconscious habit may take some time, but at the start, you need to be self-conscious about your movements. Do not turn your head around when someone says something to you to look at them. Use deliberate, purposeful movements.

Keep your shoulders back and head up as you run. Don't look down on the ground. Don't be afraid to make eye contact with people around you (and don't look down instantly when you're making eye contact, that's a sign of submission). Don't worry about taking up space. Stand about one foot-and-a-half fee apart with your hands loose. You can make sure that you take up as much space as you need to be relaxed even when you sit down. Think of " alpha male."

3. Tonality: Speak slowly and deliberately when you talk. Suppose they're interested in hearing what you've got to say. Project your voice, but you're not crying. Do not ask if she agrees if you make statements. You're not saying "right?" or "you know?" It makes you look nervous. You shouldn't handle any contact with a woman at the same time as a business meeting (except, you know, if it's a business meeting). So keep it light and fun. Laugh, but not at your own jokes. Yours only need a smirk. Do not answer it too quickly when she asks you a question, and do not give more details than needed. Never overcompensate for your shortcomings or insecurities.

When you start incorporating these components as part of your identity, girls are going to start picking them up. The awkwardness can take days, weeks, or even months to go away. But it's going to, and you're going to stop pushing these habits.

These are the bare necessities you should start thinking like a guy whose natural confidence attracts women automatically.

Remember: when you change your way of thinking, you're going to change your way of acting.

Reading other people helps you understand yourself. Now that you know how to read people, you can also avoid letting them manipulate you. Stay in control at all times. You see the signs. Use them to benefit you.

If you found this book useful, a review on Amazon is always appreciated!

MIND MASTERY SERIES

If you have come to this eBook without having read the previous parts, I suggest you do so in order to have an overall reading. Below is the correct titles, if you would like to search for them on <u>Amazon and/or Audible</u>:

<u>SECRET MANIPULATION TECHNIQUES</u>

HOW SUBLIMINAL PSYCHOLOGY CAN PERSUADE ANYONE BY APPLYING DARK PNL IN REAL-LIFE. UNDERSTANDING TACTICS & SCHEMES TO INFLUENCE PEOPLE AND CONTROL THEIR EMOTIONS

<u>HOW TO ANALYZE PEOPLE WITH DARK PSYCHOLOGY</u>

A SPEED GUIDE TO READING HUMAN PERSONALITY TYPES BY ANALYZING BODY LANGUAGE. HOW DIFFERENT BEHAVIORS ARE MANIPULATED BY MIND CONTROL

HOW TO SPEED READ PEOPLE

READING HUMAN BODY LANGUAGE TO UNDERSTAND PSYCHOLOGY AND DARK SIDE OF THE PERSONS – HOW TO ANALYZE BEHAVIORAL EMOTIONAL INTELLIGENCE FOR THE MIND CONTROL

EMOTIONAL INTELLIGENCE MASTERY

DISCOVER HOW EQ CAN MAKE YOU MORE PRODUCTIVE AT WORK AND STRENGTHEN RELATIONSHIPS. IMPROVE YOUR LEADERSHIP SKILLS TO ANALYZE & UNDERSTAND OTHER PEOPLE THROUGH EMPATHY

NLP MASTERY

HOW TO ANALYZE DARK PSYCHOLOGY TECHNIQUES TO CHANGE YOUR HABITS AND BUILD A SUCCESSFUL LIFE. ESSENTIAL GUIDE ON MIND CONTROL THROUGH CALIBRATING EMOTIONAL INTELLIGENCE AND HIDDEN EMOTIONS

*"For better enjoyment, you CAN find all this titles also in audio format, on **Audible.**"*

Do not go yet; One last thing to do…

*If you enjoyed this book or found it useful I'd be very grateful if you'd post a short review on **Amazon**. Your support really does make a difference and I read all the reviews personally so I can get your feedback and make this book even better.*

Thanks again for your support!

© Copyright 2021 by **LIAM ROBINSON**

All rights reserved

www.ingramcontent.com/pod-product-compliance
Lightning Source LLC
LaVergne TN
LVHW021110221224
799724LV00010B/709